The Dream Maker

By
Monica Hannan

Published by
E. T. NEDDER PUBLISHING
TUCSON, ARIZONA

The Book Team
Ernie Nedder, Publisher
Kathy Nedder, CFO
Monica Hannan, Author
Kate Harrison, Editor
Sharon Nicks, Designer

2007 printing

Additional copies of this publication may be purchased by sending check
or money order for $20.00 to: Theological Book Service, P.O. Box 509,
Barnhart, MO 63012. Or call toll free 1-888-247-3023. Fax: 1-800-325-9526.
E-mail: bookstore@theobooks.org. Be sure to check our Web site for a list of
other products: www.nedderpublishing.com.

Order#: 49-8
5.5 x 8.5

Individual copies: $20.00

ISBN: 1-893757-49-8

Cover photo: Miguel Angel Alvarez

Some truths are dangerous to tell, particularly in Third and Fourth World countries where war and violence are a way of life. To protect the identities of people still in danger, and out of compassion for those who would rather forget their suffering, some names and details have been changed.

"…. From everyone to whom much has been given, much will be required; and from the one to whom much has been entrusted, even more will be demanded." –Luke 12:48

ACKNOWLEDGMENTS

Your mother will read your manuscript because she is your mother. A friend will read it because he is your friend. You hope a stranger will read it simply because it's a good read.

To all of those people who read my work in progress, I say thanks. In particular, I'd like to thank Ernie Nedder, Sharon Nicks and Kate Harrison for their efforts in the final product, and my family for giving me the time to write it.

But for the one who was willing to read it, edit it, re-read it and edit it again and again, mere thanks are not enough. Therefore, I dedicate this book to Tom Hesford, my editor, mentor and friend.

The Beginning

When I was a young boy, God gave me an incredible gift. It was the gift of death. No, it was the gift of dying. It removed any doubts I ever had about God's existence, and about the reality of an afterlife.

Of course, I, too, have read all the medical explanations and fear factors and other miscellaneous reports that have been put out there to explain a near-death experience. But you know what? They are wrong. Just ask any of the millions of people to whom God has given the gift of dying. None of them, of us, will ever again be afraid of death. The importance of losing this fear cannot be overstated.

The first time author Monica Hannan said she wanted to write a biography about me, I felt embarrassed because I thought she was making fun of me. I couldn't figure out her angle, and didn't know how to respond to a punch line that I couldn't quite get. So I ignored her. A biography? I was not even 40 years old.

Several months later, Monica mentioned again that she wanted to write this biography and asked me if I would work with her on it. This time I knew she was serious, so I considered my options. I learned from an attorney friend that you can't stop someone from writing about your life if they really want to, so you can work with them or you can try to get in their way. Since I spend most of my time traveling around and working in the streets of Third and Fourth World nations, I knew that I'd have a tough time standing in her way, so I agreed to work with her. Then, the embarrassment returned.

I couldn't think of anything extraordinary that had happened to me, besides a near-drowning incident when I was very young, so I didn't know what else she and I had to talk about. She took care of that.

Then, I found myself not wanting to be the focus of a book, and especially of a biography. I mean, the work that I've done has not been my doing; it is work that has simply been done through me with the help of many, for the love of God. Any book about these experiences, or about the results of this labor, of this vocation, should focus on Christ and on his love for the poor and his desire to see that they are well.

Finally, I knew I didn't know what I would say or feel having other people read a book about my life. Pure embarrassment, of course. Absolute and complete embarrassment.

Several months ago I was speaking about Christ's love for the poor to several inner-city high school student groups in New Jersey. I told them personal experiences I'd had finding God in the streets, in the filth of the cantinas and amid the violence of war. Afterwards, several students came up and asked what they could do to find and help those who need them. Many of them wanted to go out right then and there and do something good. Surprisingly, I found myself thinking of Monica

Hannan's desire to write this book, and of how selfish I had been to try and discourage her from getting these stories told.

All of the children and the mothers you will read about in this book are real. Most are still alive, a couple have died. More than a few have been lost to the streets. Their faith and what they had to go through to live should provide tremendous encouragement for those of us who have life so much easier. I still wish I could have stayed out of this book, but if the poor and the victimized that Monica writes about here need me to be a vehicle for their stories to be told, then any personal embarrassment I feel is no price at all to be paid.

For God's love we should do all.

—*Patrick Atkinson*

I once choked on my lunch while eating Chinese food with Patrick Atkinson. He watched me struggle to clear my throat, then smiled and told me about a tickle he once had in his throat every time he ate. He said his minor coughing spells went on for months and were puzzling because he was otherwise healthy. Finally, he consulted a doctor who put a scope down his throat and found, attached to his esophagus, two parasitic worms that woke up every time he ate and grabbed at the food as it passed by on the way to his stomach.

Needless to say my enjoyment of lunch ended there, but for Patrick the story was typical. It is the kind of experience he has had dozens of times during his 20 years as a missionary in Third World countries. "If you live among the poor," he'll tell you, "you're going to get worms and lice and fleas." The fact that he tells it nonchalantly is also typical, because he doesn't see his life as extraordinary, yet it has been. He took seriously Christ's call to help the poor. He took the germ of an idea—to be a missionary and work with kids—and brought it to life in the most amazing way.

That God had a special mission in mind for Patrick Atkinson was probably obvious right from the start, although Patrick didn't see it at the time. If you ask him, he'll tell you he had a typical American childhood. In fact, he once pointed out how similar our upbringings were. He and I were both raised Catholic, we went to Catholic grade schools, and grew up not far from each other in Bismarck, N.D. He went to St. Mary's Central High School, I went to Bismarck High School, but we graduated in the same year. We also graduated from Minnesota State University Moorhead in the same year—he with degrees in social work and criminal justice, I with degrees in history and mass communications, yet our paths never crossed.

I met him for the first time more than a decade later, in 1993, long after he had moved away from his North Dakota roots. I was working as a reporter for KFYR-TV, an NBC affiliate in Bismarck. Patrick had just launched the charity that would become The GOD'S CHILD Project, and he was back home, looking for financial help. He had been a missionary in Central

America and Southeast Asia for 10 years by then, and somebody told me he had interesting stories to tell. It piqued my interest, so I arranged an interview.

At the time, I must confess, I wasn't interested in his fledgling project. What interested me was a story he told about stumbling onto a clandestine cemetery while planning a building project near Antigua. This was during Guatemala's bloody civil war, when people routinely disappeared only to turn up dead months or years later in ditches or shallow graves. After he notified authorities that he had found a mass grave, he said he became the target of an assassination attempt. He was shot at more than once, was warned by a human rights group to watch his back, and was advised by the U.S. Embassy to leave Guatemala.

As he told the story, he seemed more puzzled by the media attention that his find had caused than frightened by the obvious threat, because of course I wasn't the only reporter to pick up the story.

I asked him whether he had ever considered quitting and coming home where it was safe. He thought about it for a moment, as if the idea had not occurred to him, and then said, "No. If the good run from the bad, the bad win." It was a phrase I would hear him repeat over and over again in the years to come as I got to know him and his project better.

There were other remarkable stories involving Patrick and The GOD'S CHILD Project that I covered for KFYR—and later for magazines and newspapers. He always provided good copy because his project quickly became a success story that amazed everyone—himself most of all. He has not always been successful in everything he's tried, but he has been persistent in the face of adversity. The result has been a project that has grown to become Guatemala's largest private, comprehensive charity, supporting more than 12,000 orphaned, poverty-stricken children, mothers and homeless.

I pestered Patrick to allow me to write his story. I was convinced that others would be inspired by the way God has caused this "ordinary guy" to do extraordinary things. I wanted to show people what can happen when individuals say "yes" to God, even when they would much rather decline the invitation. Patrick always politely refused my request. Then one day he changed his mind.

He told me that he no longer objected to the idea of a book, as long as it was not so much about his life as it was about the lives that have been touched or changed for the better because he had planted a few seeds in the slums of cities like Antigua, Guatemala, and Bakasala, Malawi. He wasn't talking just about the children and families who have received assistance from The GOD'S CHILD Project, but also about the thousands of volunteers and benefactors who have been blessed because they also answered God's call.

In those three years I've conducted dozens of interviews, not just with him, but with those who know him, grew up with him or work with him. I filled countless hours of audio tape and asked him to tell the same stories over and over again so that I could recreate them accurately. I have asked him to translate hundreds of pages of Guatemalan documents, court records and newspaper articles from Spanish to English, which forced him to relive moments I'm sure he would rather forget. He did this bravely and without complaint (at least not much complaint). He's hollered at me more than once, I've seen his eyes well up with tears more than once and we've laughed a lot. Many times he has submitted to interviews while battling illness— once from a hospital bed, and through it all, he has always kept sight of his main goal, of aiding the poor.

"Most people want to help," he often says. "They just don't know how. I give them a way."

Monica Hannan
2005

CHAPTER ONE

San Pedro Las Huertas
ANTIGUA, GUATEMALA
July 4, 2000

Three-year-old Carlos Hermenegildo Chuy Monroy was nearly asleep in his family's rented house—a shack constructed of concrete blocks with a packed-dirt floor and a rusted tin roof, on a farm in San Pedro Las Huertas, Antigua, Guatemala. Although it was crowded, the family was lucky to have it. It meant that Carlitos' (little Carlos') father, Marcelino, had a job. He was a caretaker on the estate of the former governor of the province of Sacatepequez , and it was a responsibility that he did not take lightly. It put food in his children's bellies, and offered some chance for his family's future.

Three beds lined the walls of the single room. Carlitos shared one of the beds with his little brother, 2-year-old Gustavo, and his 6-year-old sister, Maria Magaly. His uncle slept on the second bed, his parents shared the third.

It was quiet on this mild July night. The children were lulled by the low sounds of a radio playing on a shelf overhead, the conversation of their parents standing just outside the doorway, the rhythmic drone of their uncle's snoring. At some point, Carlitos heard his mother walk back inside. Maria Luisa breathed a soft sigh as she lowered herself onto the side of the narrow bed and removed her sandals. Eight-and-a-half months pregnant, she felt heavy, everything an effort.

She looked up in alarm at the sudden, sharp sound of her husband arguing with somebody on the road in front of the house. She thought she recognized the voice of the man who yelled back, but she wasn't certain until she heard the word "motorcycle." A feeling of dread swept over her as she rose and hurried to the door.

Carlitos was wide-awake now, also listening to the argument outside, his heart hammering in his chest. He didn't understand everything his father said, but he was certain of one thing. Marcelino was both angry and afraid. Carlitos also recognized the voice of the other man. It was Juan Pablo Ocampo Alcala, called El Pato (The Duck). He was notorious in the neighborhood for his criminal connections and infamous for his violent outbursts. El Pato had been heard to brag about the men he had killed and the people he had hurt. He was offering Marcelino a bribe, 2,000 quetzals (about $50), if he would simply look the other way while El Pato stole a motorcycle and a few other things from the estate.

"After all, he is my brother-in-law," El Pato reasoned. "He owes me."

There was bitterness in El Pato, perhaps born of jealousy and deep-seated feelings of inadequacy. He hadn't gotten much when he married the governor's sister. He felt he deserved more.

He had friends in high places, certainly, and those whom he couldn't buy with bribes he sometimes simply removed from the picture. But his brother-in-law possessed something that El Pato lacked, something that no amount of money could buy—respectability. It was something to be desired above all else. His wife's family name had not bought it for him, so he had won respect of a different sort, "respect" gained through intimidation and fear. People glanced up when they saw him coming—he was certainly well known, but somehow that recognition was a hollow victory.

Blinded by his anger, El Pato now saw Marcelino as another barrier, somebody else standing in the way of what he wanted.

Marcelino saw the look in El Pato's eye, saw the assault rifle he held in his hands and was frightened, but he refused to back down. He had worked too long and too hard for this job. He didn't want to lose it. He ordered El Pato to leave at once, hoping his loud, angry voice would be weapon enough to discourage the man and make him go away. His eyes grew wide when El Pato raised the rifle and took aim.

At the sound of their father's angry shout, Carlitos and his sister sat up. They could see the outline of their mother's face in the faint light from the doorway, and they could see her hesitate at the threshold, unsure of what to do. That it was dangerous to cross El Pato was something they all understood. He had come once before, a month earlier, making the same demands.

Marcelino had said no then, and El Pato had promised he would be back.

"Jose!" Maria Luisa called to her brother, still asleep inside. "Wake up!"

"What is it?" he mumbled sleepily.

"El Pato!"

Responding to the name, and to his sister's frantic tone, Jose Baudilio Monroy Reyes sprang from the bed and was on his way outside when the first shot was fired. Maria Luisa, standing in the doorway, screamed as her husband slumped forward into the dirt.

"What are you doing!" she cried, as all of the children bolted from the bed and ran toward her. "You killed him!"

El Pato seemed not to hear her, but instead, advanced on Jose, who had come to a standstill in the middle of the yard.

"No!" the young man cried, holding his hands out, but El Pato never stopped walking. He fired his automatic rifle again, and watched with satisfaction as Jose fell. Maria Luisa screamed again and finally, El Pato noticed her. She tried to back away, shoving her children behind her into the house, never taking her eyes from his face, but he followed her. He aimed his rifle at her pregnant abdomen and fired deliberately. After she fell he shot her again, then slammed the butt of his rifle into her face over and over again, her blood splattering onto his clothes. Maria had attempted to shield her children with her body, and they now lay under her where she lay dying. As her daughter, Maria

Magaly, tried to crawl away, El Pato took aim at her, firing once. She lay still. Glancing up, he saw Carlitos escape out the back door. No matter. It was sport, really, a chance to do a little hunting. El Pato paused long enough to notice baby Gustavo, still partially covered by his mother's fallen form, and shot him in the head before following Carlitos through the rear of the house.

Carlitos didn't get far before El Pato leaned out into the darkness and fired at him, too. The little boy could feel the bullet rocket into his abdomen, although at first there was no pain. The force of the blow knocked him down, but he sprang up again and ran into a nearby cornfield, hoping to hide as El Pato stalked him, stopping every once in a while to listen. Twice more he shot at the boy, hitting him in the abdomen again, and then the buttocks. On the third shot, Carlitos fell. He curled into a ball, and struggled not to cry, cough, or even breathe. El Pato listened once more, then wandered back inside the house, rummaging around for anything of value.

He found little that was of any use. He liked being in the house, though. He liked to look at the blood, to see his handiwork and know he was powerful enough to create this kind of chaos and death. He took time to count the bodies. A good night's work, even if he didn't have much of value to show for it. He rummaged for a moment more before walking back out into the yard, stooping to dig through Marcelino's pockets, then raising his fist in triumph. He had found the motorcycle keys. He gave the dead man one last kick, then stepped over him and swung his leg onto the motorcycle. He was thirsty, and knew just where to go to find a drink. He fired up the engine and headed back toward town.

Not far down the road, he stopped under the lights of a bar owned by a foreigner, an American. A beer was just what he needed.

"Hello my friend," he called out as he walked into the nearly deserted bar. The American glanced up. This particular customer usually meant trouble.

"A beer," El Pato said as he leaned onto the bar. The American saw that the man was covered in blood, as if he had walked through a red mist. He saw, but he said nothing. Questions weren't necessary. El Pato volunteered the information.

"I've just killed six people," he said smugly. He took a sip from his beer. "I like the smell of hot blood, don't you?"

The bar owner didn't want to know anything. The last thing he wanted was trouble. He remained silent, edging away.

"Perhaps I could leave this with you?" El Pato said, thrusting his rifle forward, but the American refused to take it. He raised his hands in front of him and shook his head.

"No? All right then. Who knows, I might need it again," he said with a vaguely threatening gesture, then smiled at the look of fear that crossed the American's face. He drained his beer, picked up his rifle and walked out. The American breathed deeply with relief when he heard the motorcycle roar to life out front.

From his hiding place in the cornfield, Carlitos listened carefully. He did not hear anybody coming for him. Perhaps it was a trick. Perhaps as soon as he moved, El Pato would shoot him again. He lay as long as he could, but by now a burning pain was gripping his gut, and dizziness was beginning to overtake him. He couldn't be still any longer. He pushed himself up onto all fours and crawled toward a neighbor's house on the other side of the cornfield. The journey seemed to take forever, but finally, he made it to the door of the shack. It was then that he began to cry as he pounded with his tiny fists.

"El Pato! El Pato is hitting my mama. He wants to kill me!" he wailed, before his neighbor scooped him up, thrust a hand over his mouth and carried him inside.

"Shh!" he whispered to Carlitos. "Be quiet, or he'll hear you and come after us, too." He laid the blood-soaked child on a bed, then watched from the window, waiting for what seemed an eternity, needing to be certain that El Pato was really gone and would not come back.

"Do you think it's safe?" he whispered to his wife.

"It's quiet," she responded. "If you don't go soon it will be too late," she said, nodding at the circle of blood that grew around the child.

"OK, I'll go," the man said, and slipped quietly from his house. Once on the road, he started to run, and didn't stop until he made it to the fire station, where he summoned help. By the time police arrived, Carlitos was in shock. His parents, uncle and sister were dead, and his little brother Gustavo had lapsed into a coma.

CHAPTER TWO

The Dreamer Center

SAN FELIPE SLUMS, ANTIGUA, GUATEMALA

Nov. 1, 2000

"Lots of children have told me their nightmares. About how they've been beaten, tortured, shot and used by some really sick people. They talk about the time they saw their brothers kidnapped, or how they left to hoe corn one morning and stumbled across their father's body that same night. I don't try to remember too many of their stories, though. I can't. I might go crazy and would certainly never sleep again at night. My years of experience with tortured children have taught me to remain outside of their nightmares. It's only from there that I can keep them safe when they try to venture back in...."

—Patrick Atkinson,
founder of The GOD'S CHILD Project,
in a letter to friends.

———————————

Patrick Atkinson rarely sits down. One gets the impression that he hops out of bed each morning with a "to-do" list in one hand and a diet cola in the other, the one vice that his tortured liver still allows him. He's had hepatitis more than once, which means he takes a cautious approach to food and drink, but he needs a caffeine jolt to get him up and running. His doctors have told him that the liver has a remarkable capacity to heal, but it's a bad idea for him to overdo it. For that reason, he doesn't drink alcohol and is careful about taking any medications that aren't strictly necessary, although he has a small handful that he must take each day to keep himself upright and moving. Drugs like anti-malarials, and anti-parasitics, which he dutifully downs with a chaser of Diet Pepsi Con Limon. He has been told by well-meaning friends that the constant barrage of chemicals from the soft drinks can't be good for him, either.

"But then, as much as I travel, the daily changes in water will probably kill me long before this stuff will," he says with a smile, opening his second can of the day. It's 8:30 a.m., time to greet his staff and come up with a plan of action. I am on the scene to cover a series of stories for KFYR-TV, and also to observe him at work. To "live the life," is how he put it to me when we made arrangements for my visit. The meeting is brief. It ends with a prayer and his staff of volunteers and paid employees scatters.

Patrick concentrates on the stack of bills piled in front of him, but it's not easy. He is constantly interrupted by the ringing phone and the steady stream of people who stop at his desk with problems that need to be solved. It's immediately apparent that he is the main cog that runs the machine.

Mixing in with the general hubbub is the sound of a child wailing in the hallway. At first, Patrick manages to ignore it. His office in The Dreamer Center complex is always crowded with women and children. Tears aren't unusual. But this child's cries are hard to dismiss. Patrick wonders aloud why the mother doesn't take the poor kid down to the clinic near the main gate of The Dreamer Center. They must have passed it when they came in. Perhaps the doctor was busy and they have been forced to wait. The breezeway outside his office door is a cool spot. It opens onto a rooftop courtyard, shaded by trees and furnished with tables and chairs. He likes to sit there himself when the office pace exhausts him. The view of the nearby volcanoes, rising up through the clouds, always reminds him of what he's doing here in what sometimes seems to be a God-forsaken land. The beauty of the mountains is in sharp contrast to the neighboring San Felipe slums, where ramshackle dwellings dot the twisting pathways along the steep hillside behind The Dreamer Center complex.

The Dreamer Center itself is built on the remains of a garbage dump—land nobody wanted before Patrick claimed it for his growing charity for destitute children and homeless families. Now it has become the Guatemalan headquarters for The GOD'S CHILD Project, constructed through donations and with the help of international volunteers. Its humble beginnings are there for all to see, in photographs adorning the walls of the center.

The trash on the site was once 15-feet thick, covered over by silt that ran down the mountainsides during the rainy season. Long grass had grown in, in patches here and there, but the garbage had still been visible underneath, moldering in smelly heaps. Along with those pictures were the images he captured of former scavengers of the dump—children and families with no hope. It was their eyes, dull and lifeless, bereft of dreams, that had first captured his heart. When he received a grant from Dreamer Ministries of Plano, Texas, to purchase the grounds and build a Guatemalan base of operations for The GOD'S CHILD Project, it seemed prophetic, so Patrick named the new facility The Dreamer Center. He designed a simple work space, the desks separated from one another by bamboo and potted papaya trees into areas that he calls living sanctuaries, places where people can work in peace, without walls. But they rarely have time to notice their surroundings. Growth has been rapid.

In time the complex has grown to include a medical clinic and dental clinic, kitchens, classrooms, a library, a chapel, courtyards, an amphitheater, and an office area where a small staff coordinates the activities of volunteers from all over the world.

Patrick is on the phone when his assistant, Freddy Maldonado, leans over and whispers in his ear. There is a man outside who belongs to the child who won't stop wailing.

Patrick glances with momentary regret at the list of phone calls he has yet to make and at the pile of paperwork he has been putting off for days. He shoves them aside and follows Freddy out. He nearly trips over what at first glance appears to be a small bundle of rags.

A second look reveals a little boy, curled into a tiny ball on the hallway floor just outside the office door. He is clutching his mid-section, howling, tears streaming down his dirty face.

The man who stands beside the child, trying in vain to comfort him, is clearly exhausted. The boy is obviously in agony. It is a difficult thing to watch.

"Patrick," says Freddy, "this is Luis Fernando Chuy, and this little guy here is his cousin, Carlitos."

The story comes tumbling out: Luis Fernando tells him that Carlitos was shot three times, and that the bullets had torn up his insides. He was stabilized at an emergency center in July, but there seemed little else that Guatemalan doctors could do for him. It has been four months, and the child is not getting better. If anything, his condition is growing worse.

Luis picks Carlitos up and shows Patrick a catheter that pokes through the skin to the right of his pubic area. The catheter is connected to a bag filled with bloody urine. The cousin explains that the boy cannot urinate normally and is in extreme pain caused by bladder and bowel spasms that hit every 20 minutes or so, day and night.

"Every time I hear about another agency, I take him there, but everywhere I go they tell me 'no,'" Luis says. "I think they are afraid of the drug connection—of El Pato."

He explains that the doctors who saw Carlitos in Antigua did all they could. There is a specialist in Guatemala City who is willing to examine him, but he has demanded payment first.

"I have no money." Luis miserably admits.

Patrick understands. Here is a boy who is dying, in a country full of sad stories, and nobody wants to waste precious resources on a lost cause. Furthermore, nobody wants to cross El Pato. As Luis' story unfolds, Patrick remembers the news articles he has read about the massacre of the Chuy Monroy family. The reports said that witnesses who had heard or seen something on the night that little Carlitos was shot were already disappearing, or had developed amnesia. Key pieces of evidence—the murder weapon, the bloodstained clothes—have disappeared from evidence lockers. El Pato has powerful friends and access to money, a dangerous combination in Guatemala. Carlitos is perhaps the only living witness. Associating with him could prove deadly.

But Patrick is willing to take the risk. To refuse does not seem to occur to him.

He gives Luis' shoulder a quick squeeze, and sends the two of them down to The Dreamer Center clinic for an initial evaluation. While Freddy accompanies them downstairs, Patrick returns to his desk, shoves the bills and paperwork into a drawer, and opens a new file. He writes "Carlitos" across the top, picks up the phone and dials the number for Dr. Kevin Mickelson, an emergency room physician at St. Alexius Medical Center in Bismarck, N.D. As he dials, he glances up.

"I think I know somebody who can be counted on to help," he says. He waits for a connection. "Have you ever seen a more beautiful kid?" he continues. "From the looks of him, I'd say he needs serious medical intervention right away, or he won't stand a chance. And do you know what's really sad? If he lives, and if he ever sees the inside of a classroom, he probably won't be the only kid in his class who's been shot."

Dr. Mickelson does not answer, so Patrick leaves a callback request before calling one of his contacts in the Guatemalan Attorney General's office. A brief conversation ensues. It is clear that getting Carlitos out of the country quickly will not be an easy task. For one thing, Patrick says, the child likely was born at home and has no birth certificate, and as an orphan, he has no parents who can vouch for him. His cousin's family has taken him into their house, a very humble dwelling on the outskirts of Antigua. Nobody had expected Carlitos to live very long, and yet, weeks later he keeps fighting. His constant pain is wearing on his new family, though, Patrick can see that, and he knows that caring for a sick child must be particularly difficult in the Altotenango slums where Luis lives.

When Carlitos finishes at the clinic, Patrick sends his assistants, Javier Alvarado and Richard, the latter a volunteer from Canada, to check out their living conditions while he waits for a report from the project doctor.

Luis lives with his wife and his own three children, in a house set back from the road down a narrow alleyway. It is not a house at all, but a series of lean-tos made of cornstalks and discarded trash. Clothing and blankets are hung on lines at regular intervals inside the cramped, dark space, serving two purposes. They provide some privacy between sleeping and living areas, and they eliminate the need for a separate place to store clothes. There are light sockets running along a crisscross of cords overhead, but no bulbs are in them. The family uses candles for light.

The cooking area is in a separate covered shelter across the courtyard. There is running water there, in a broken, concrete sink—a luxury by Guatemalan standards, but the plumbing is malfunctioning and the water has pooled onto the dirt floor, creating sticky mud which the family chickens track through, while adding their own waste to the mix. The baby of the family, a boy still in diapers, crawls around in the slime, sharing space with the chickens and a puppy that one of the children has dragged home. His older sister, a child not yet in her teens, is in charge on this day, and does her best to keep the baby out of the filth, without much success. In his hand is an old spoon and a rusty can, which serve as toys.

Carlitos shows Javier where he sleeps, in one of the beds with Luis, who is forced to get up repeatedly in the night when the child cries out from his spasms, frequently soiling himself. Keeping him clean is a huge challenge. Their bathroom is a latrine in an alcove. There is no shower, only the cold water at the sink. Still, Luis does his best by the child. He explains that he sits up with him night after night. He tells Javier he has lost his job because of it. He has high hopes that Patrick can help.

CHAPTER THREE

When I was a small child, I used to sneak into my sister's room and move the three tall mirrors on her dresser. The opposing reflections would suddenly form an illusionary hallway with an infinite number of exits. Sitting and staring for what seemed like hours, I would dream about what would happen if I could enter this magical hallway, and leave at will through any of its limitless, mirrored doors.

— From the personal letters of Patrick Atkinson

That Patrick would turn to friends in North Dakota for help is natural. It is where he has always turned when trouble comes knocking. Ask him to talk about his boyhood, and he will do his best to convince you that it was perfectly ordinary, and in many ways, it was.

It was hard to find a more idyllic place to grow up than North Dakota in 1959, the year that Patrick was born. Sweeping changes were fast approaching — the turbulent '60s and '70s were still ahead — but those changes were slow in coming to the Marge and Myron Atkinson home on West Avenue B in Bismarck. The house was large and welcoming, with a wide, screened-in front porch and a looping driveway. The tree-lined street rang with the shouts of children playing, screen doors slamming and neighbors chatting to one another over hedges. As he remembers it, kids scrambled in and out of each other's houses all summer long while mothers up and down the block kept up a constant supply of Kool Aid and peanut butter and jelly sandwiches. People seldom locked their doors. Crime was almost non-existent. There was one church for every 800 souls, and on Sundays those houses of worship were filled.

The Atkinsons were conservative Catholics, fiercely loyal and protective of the family name, and with good reason. They had roots in the community that ran deep on both sides. Myron's mother could remember when Bismarck was a brand new town, home to only 2,500 people—little more than a railroad stop on the way to opportunities in the West. Myron's father was a city auditor. Marge's parents had established themselves in business, starting up a shoe store. Myron and Marjory met as children, although they didn't date until later. After Myron finished a law degree at the University of North Dakota law school, they married and started their family.

Myron Atkinson discovered fairly quickly that he didn't care much for law, but like his father before him, he had a real talent for business. It wasn't long before he had made a name for himself in Bismarck, developing properties. Marjory did her part by caring for her large brood of seven children and taking an active role in church and civic duties. If you needed something done, someone to chair a committee or organize a Scout drive,

Marjory Atkinson was the woman to call. She ran her home with a firm, yet loving efficiency, and was a good partner for her husband, serving as the proper hostess when he brought business people home. Theirs was a household in constant motion, full of children, friends and extended family.

The dinner table was the place where Myron kept track of his growing family, finding out how they did in school that day, discussing family business, talking about events happening around them. Not attending the family dinner was usually not an option, especially when the children were young.

Sometimes the hours spent around the dining room table were an agony for Patrick, who was always a wiggler anyway, and always in the middle of something vital when he was called to supper. Summers were the worst because he could hear his friends calling to one another, playing in the street outside, and he longed to join them. The children had been taught to wait to take their seats until Myron came to the table. He would lead the family in grace and then, for Patrick at least, eating always seemed to take an eternity. And that was just the ordinary nights. Meals on special occasions, like birthdays, lasted even longer. And after dinner they almost always said a decade of the rosary together before they could be on their way. It was never Patrick's favorite part of the evening, and when he led the prayers, a task that was rotated among family members, he usually tried to rush them a little bit, which would elicit a warning glance from his mother.

Patrick would remember those family meal times as difficult, yet formative, and would later say that they probably played a big role in his and his siblings' successes. They taught him the importance of family interaction and parent involvement in a child's life.

"If you know that somebody really cares, that somebody will be checking up on you at the end of the day, checking your grades, asking about your friends and your plans for the evening, you try a little bit harder," he'd say. The importance of that family contact and interaction was ingrained in him; and yet, if you ask his parents, they'll tell you that Patrick was the one child who successfully broke away from that mold.

By the time he was in junior high school, the fiercely private Patrick was frequently absent from the family table because his activities kept him so busy. He simply refused to be harnessed, and because he was respectful and stayed out of trouble, his parents finally just looked the other way, accepting the truth, which was that they couldn't control him. He had mastered the art of passive resistance, making himself scarce to avoid conflicts and questions. His father, at times a stern disciplinarian, would try to force the issue, but in the end, Patrick always managed to go his own way.

"They finally saw the futility in trying to tie him down," his brother Tim remembers. He mentions with regret the times he also tried to force Patrick to conform. "I was the oldest, and I knew that it bothered my parents that he went his own way so often, so I wanted to make him behave like everybody else. I even got a little physical with him at one point, before I realized that he was just not like the rest of us. I've always felt bad about that. We see now that he simply danced to a different tune. We have a saying in our family that everybody understands to this day. Patrick is just being Patrick." And while Patrick doesn't care much for the phrase, he will admit he got away with things the other children simply didn't.

"You were never really sure what was going on with him, but the outcome was always good," his mother recalls. She relates how Patrick came home one evening and mentioned in passing that he was being recognized by the Boy Scouts, in case they wanted to be there. "He downplayed it so much that we almost didn't attend," Marjory recalls with a laugh. "Imagine our surprise that night when we arrived at a ceremony in his honor. He was receiving the Red Lantern Award, the highest honor in scouting, usually reserved for adults. He was just a kid, and he had organized a scout troop for mentally handicapped children, so that they could participate in scouting. He was in his mid teens."

It was impossible not to be proud of a kid like that, but family members will tell you that Myron really didn't understand his son. He supported his work, but when Patrick was a young man, Myron thought he was going through a phase and that eventually he would settle down to a more normal life. Patrick himself will tell you that in his younger days, if there was one person he was eager to impress, it was his father. The trouble was, Patrick was also listening to an inner voice that was pushing him in a different direction, a voice he found impossible to ignore.

Most of his early successes came at school and church. As a child, Patrick found his Catholic faith both fascinating and comforting. He loved the tradition of it, the sense of belonging to something larger than himself. It was something he always felt when he participated in Mass or church events. On the other hand, he never got too hung up on rules.

"I can remember thinking as a kid that he was something of a hypocrite," Tim says, "because here he'd be working to help others or getting involved with Christian youth groups, and then he'd sleep in some Sundays and miss Mass, and it didn't seem to bother him. But I came to realize he was not so much religious, as deeply spiritual. Because, at the same time, I would sometimes come home late after a night out with my friends, pass Patrick's doorway and see that he had fallen asleep while kneeling beside his bed, in a position that would show he'd been praying. Even back then he ran himself ragged and didn't stop until he simply dropped. He could fall asleep just like that," Tim adds, snapping his fingers. "For him, Christianity was a way of life, not a Sunday thing. He was actually living it, even back then."

He was never worried about stylish clothes or having the latest thing. He would give his pocket money to the poor and thought it was cool to dress in clothes from the local thrift store, and yet he was popular with other kids. He was chosen twice as the St. Mary's High School class president. He was on the varsity wrestling team, and was a member of various clubs. He was usually surrounded by groups of friends with whom he keeps in touch to this day, and yet he was always careful not to give away too much of himself. Friends would say in letters that they found him delightful company, but essentially unreachable. Ask Patrick why that is and he'll look puzzled, tell you he has wonderful friends, that he's just like everybody else, that he's not unreachable at all. But in the next breath, he'll also admit that he hesitates to get too close to people because he doesn't want them to interfere with what God wants from him.

"If I have a date with my girlfriend and I get the call that I'm needed in Malawi, Africa, I'm going to Malawi. That's how it is, and not too many people will stand for that over the long haul," he says. It's a characteristic that has led to a lonely life, but he doesn't dwell on it. That he felt singled out for a specific mission was evident from grade school on. Patrick also believes his need for others is tempered by the fact that God has always been there for him as a special friend. He has always talked to him as he would any other companion, keeping up running dialogues. He is frequently left waiting for answers, but he has faith that eventually, those answers will come.

He had many questions about matters of faith, and about life and death in his grade school years. He always listened closely in class or in church when matters of doctrine and faith were discussed, which was often.

He attended Cathedral of the Holy Spirit Grade School, just down the street from his house. Catholic school classrooms in those days were large. Classes of 35 and 40 children were not unusual, and yet, Patrick distinguished himself. In addition to his studies and his Scouting, in his later grade school years he led the altar boys, organizing the schedule and even coming up with incentives to encourage more boys to participate in altar serving.

In fact, it was during one of those incentives, a summer campout that he had organized as a reward for altar servers, that Patrick had an experience that he later would say was pivotal in determining the direction his life would take.

It happened the summer he turned 13, the year he graduated from Cathedral Eighth Grade.

He remembers it as if it were yesterday, and he can still tell the story in minute detail. He had been looking forward to the campout weekend all year, and he remembers he was still up in his room, just stuffing his flashlight and canteen into his backpack and forcing the zipper closed when he heard his father's car pull into the driveway. That was his cue to get to the table.

———————

Patrick raced down the stairs, tossed his gear onto the porch and joined his brothers and sisters in the dining room.

"Patrick, you're late," his mother said quietly. If there was one thing he loved to do, she knew, it was to pack a sleeping bag onto the back of his bike and head for the water. She worried about him when he went off on his own, but she trusted him. Even at 13, Patrick was one of the most resourceful people she knew, although she says he was a bit of a daredevil. He was never content to just climb a tree. He had to climb it all the way to the top, and crawl out onto the narrowest branches, just to see if he could touch the tips. He thought nothing of leaping from roof to roof if the houses were close together, or swinging from a tree rope over a fence. She was always saying, "Patrick, come down from there before you break your neck." And he did have some close calls. She was forever running him to the emergency room with one injury or another. And yet he was responsible, too. He never got into serious trouble; and while she didn't always understand him, she was proud of him. Besides, their town was one of the safest places on earth.

While Myron washed up, Patrick remembers he kept his eye on the clock and shifted from foot to foot. When his father finally breezed in and took his place at the head of the table, there was still grace to get through before Marjory could serve. Patrick knew it didn't matter how fast he ate, his getaway was delayed by the slowest eater, usually his little brother, the then three-year-old Paul.

But finally, they were finished. He asked to be excused and the request was granted. His parents were glad of his involvement with the altar boys at the church.

The annual campout was the perfect boys' adventure. On this year the boys had staked out their spot at Apple Creek, a tree-lined, quiet place not far from Bismarck. They had rented tents, which were already in various stages of assembly by the time Patrick and his best friend, Gerard Hagen, arrived. The boys got to work and soon had their own tent up beside the others, and had laid out their sleeping bags and gear. It was a muggy night, they were hot and sweaty, and more than ready for a swim when they finished their work, but by then it was getting dark, so they had to wait until the next morning. They settled for ghost stories around the campfire and good-natured teasing before bedding down for the night.

The next morning, though, they headed for the water right after breakfast, eager to board the metal canoes they had rented for the occasion. They chose teams and climbed in.

"Life jackets, boys!" called Don Kadrmas, one of the adult chaperones on the trip. The command was met with mild grumbling, but no serious arguments. Apple Creek wasn't very big, but it was deep in the middle, well over the boys' heads. And since the point of the game was to try to sink the other team's canoe, they knew that lifejackets were important.

Patrick strapped his bright orange jacket on and cinched it up tight—not that he thought he'd need it. Even though he was one of the oldest boys there, he was also one of the smallest at only 72 pounds, which meant that his job in the game was to stay with the canoe and try to paddle it away when all of the other boys jumped in the water and tried to rock the opposing team's boat until it sank. He was usually successful at evasive action and often didn't even get wet unless he wanted to.

At first his team appeared to be winning, although it was difficult to tell with all of the splashing and bailing. The bows of the canoes had just bumped when the boys began pouring over the sides, grabbing onto their opponents' boat and rocking it back and forth so that it took on water. The first team to sink a canoe would be declared the winner. Patrick was tossed from side to side, but managed to stay on board. He paddled rapidly away from the others and then tried bailing, but he quickly lost ground and realized there was no hope of keeping the craft afloat. So he did what he often did at that point. He abandoned ship. As he jumped over the side, though, he felt something tug at his leg, and remembered that he had tied the canoe's rope around his ankle so he wouldn't have to swim so far to retrieve the boat. Too late, he realized his mistake. As the rope pulled against his ankle, he could feel the tug of the heavy metal boat as it slipped beneath the surface of the water. It was sinking slowly to the bottom, and pulling him down along with it. He wasn't concerned at first.

"Hey! Help!" he yelled to the other boys, but they were busy pushing each other's heads under the water and splashing. He noted that the other canoe had also gone under, so his side had won after all. They were busy congratulating themselves and everybody was yelling. Nobody paid him the slightest attention. With a growing sense of urgency, Patrick turned toward the shore, waving wildly and calling for help, but the adults didn't turn to look. In a panic, he tried to free his ankle by shaking it back and forth. When that didn't work, he tried to reach down, but the lifejacket that he had tied on so carefully held him upright. He wasn't strong enough to overcome its buoyant effect. He bobbed like a cork for several seconds more, but the canoe weighed more than he did, and his head finally slipped beneath the water. His heart pounding, he pulled against the drag of the big metal boat until his head broke the surface again, but he only had time for a quick breath before he went back under. Twice more he was able to push to the surface and grab at air, but he was tiring. He made one more unsuccessful attempt at reaching down to untie his leg, and then tried again to un-strap the lifejacket, which was faithfully holding him upright. His fingers were becoming clumsy and his progress was slow. He peered up, hoping that help was on the way, but he saw only the rays of the early morning sun streaking through the water. Finally he did the only thing he could do. He released the stale air in his lungs, choked momentarily on water, then stopped struggling.

Patrick was afraid at first, but his panic was soon replaced by a sense of peace and calm. It was just as if he were a tiny baby, held safely in his mother's arms. As warmth spread through his limbs, he became aware of a woman's voice, one that he heard not with his ears, but from somewhere inside his mind.

"Don't worry, I have you," the voice said. He began to see little scenes from his life, as if he were at the movies—perfectly ordinary things–sitting with his brother drinking cold Coke on the dock by the river; scratching his name in the wet cement behind his house; his first day of school. He even saw himself as an infant lying on the rug at his parents' feet, looking up at them as they hosted a gathering. He could see the ice in their glasses, could feel the happiness in their discussion. He felt the cold draft on the back of his tiny neck. He felt the same fears and joys, the same confusion, the same love he must have felt back then. It went on for a long time–yet it also took no time at all.

When it was finished, he heard a different voice, a man's this time, tell him, "You've lived well." Then there was a physical pull. Patrick felt as if he were a hand pulled from a glove. He suddenly found himself outside of his body, hovering about 15 feet above the surface of Apple Creek, looking at himself beneath the surface of the water. It didn't frighten him so much as interest him. He saw his hair floating in a cloud around his head, his arms outstretched. He noted that his eyes were closed, his mouth opened to the water. He saw that he had managed to unstrap only one of the clips on the lifejacket.

He barely had time to notice those things before he felt himself moving rapidly through a vast space, heading somewhere, toward some unknown destination. He didn't wonder what was ahead, because what was passing by was far too fascinating. Where was he? In a tunnel? He thought so, but there were no limits to it, no sides that he could see, and yet he felt it was tunnel-like. He sensed time passing, as if he were moving rapidly through the ages, watching as countless generations flew by. He heard fleeting sounds—a chanting choir of thousands, a man speaking a language he didn't understand. He heard a ringing bell, saw lights and shapes that he couldn't begin to identify. There was a lot of noise at first, but it gradually diminished, and was eventually replaced by a peaceful quiet. In the distance he could see a curtain of mist. As he drew closer he could see shapes moving in the mist, like people seen through a dense fog. He didn't know who they were, but they seemed to be waiting for him, as if to greet him. They were turning toward him, looking at him, beckoning. In his mind, he felt their welcoming warmth. Who were they? Finally, he caught sight of his destination. It was a bright light–a tremendous ball of heat that he somehow understood was pure, absolute love. It felt limitless. He wanted to be a part of it, to be absorbed by it. He somehow knew that if he passed through that curtain of mist there would be no turning back, and yet he yearned to pass through it, to be a part of it forever. He just knew that this was how it worked.

Then he heard another man's voice, gentle but authoritative, say, "You have to go back. It's not your time," and he stopped moving forward.

As quickly as that it was over. He felt himself sucked backwards at a tremendous speed and was absorbed back into his body more quickly than the time it took to blink. He could suddenly feel the cold of the water, the burn of his lungs, the tug of the rope–he spotted Fr. Ed Wehner looking down at him through the water, felt his friend Perry Kadrmas' hands pulling him roughly to the shore. He was surrounded by chaos, pushed onto his stomach, everybody shouting and running while he vomited water and took deep breaths, coughing and sputtering. As soon as he could fill his lungs with air, he burst into tears.

"Don kept telling me not to be scared," remembers Patrick. "He kept patting me on the back and saying, 'You're OK. You're safe now.' But I couldn't stop crying." Finally, he says, Don's look of relief had turned to concern again. Father Wehner suggested that they call his parents.

Patrick didn't want that. He says he suddenly knew, instinctively, that everybody needed to believe he was OK, that everything was the same as it had always been. He caught a strange look on Gerard's face–a puzzled anxiety–and it stopped his tears. He understood, somehow, that he couldn't tell Gerard or Don, or anybody else what had really happened. They would never understand. They would look at him differently. Nor could he tell them that he cried not from fear, but from devastation, because he had not wanted to return.

Talking about the experience nearly 30 years later, Patrick says, "I wasn't certain what that near-death experience meant, but when it was over I was absolutely sure of three things: that God existed, that life goes on after death, and that I had been sent back because there was something else that I had to do. I never doubted any of these from that moment on."

He spent many hours that summer and in the months and years that followed, wondering just what had happened and why he had been sent back. He never spoke of it, but the memory of his drowning experience and the journey that followed it always filled him with a sense of purpose, and helped to deepen his faith.

During his late teens, his summers were spent volunteering as a counselor at a camp for Jewish children in Maine. It was there that he had his first taste of working with kids. They came from all walks of life, but Patrick recognized the same need in all of them. They had their own insecurities, their own private griefs. He spent hours talking with the kids, and also with the other counselors—young people his own age or a little older.

Most of his fellow counselors took home with them valuable insights they had gained during those summer months. They resolved to do their best to weave their strong beliefs into their daily lives and eventual careers as lawyers, stockbrokers and business leaders. But for Patrick it was different. He felt that serving God, to go where God led him, *was* the career he was meant to have. He also felt sure that his work was going to be difficult.

He was drawn to books about missionaries working in the inner city—books about John Bosco, a priest who worked in Italy's inner cities at the turn of the 19th century. He also gathered inspiration from David Wilkerson's *The Cross and the Switchblade*. He thought he knew where he had to go, but he didn't know how to get there. God took care of that, though.

During the last summer Patrick worked in Maine, he had a long lay-over in Chicago's O'Hare International Airport. He was flipping through a magazine when he read an article about a small program that worked with street children in New York City's Hells Kitchen. Before he even finished the article he knew that was where he had to go.

CHAPTER FOUR

A letter home

New York City
March 24, 1982

Dear Mom and Dad,

Yesterday was a pretty tough day. I took a phone call from some kid who ran away from a community upstate. He was all of 14 years old. He came to the city because he was ticked off at his parents, but of course he had no idea where he was going. He came up out of the subway to find himself in one of the ugliest, deadliest parts of town. He was lucky at first. Some lady spotted him, took him by the hand to a phone booth and made him call us at the shelter. We picked him up and brought him here. I told the kid to stay put, to watch TV, to not move while we sorted things out, but he didn't listen. He went out the door with one of the older kids and hasn't come back. That was 36 hours ago. I went looking for him, but let's face it, by now that kid has probably been drugged, raped and beaten up. Some pervert will be buying a video of the whole thing tomorrow down in Times Square for 200 bucks. Man, what am I doing here? I wonder if I could get a job on Richter's farm in Menoken if I came back home for the summer...

New York City has changed a great deal since the early '80s, when Patrick first stepped off the train at Grand Central Station.

"It's a lot cleaner, for one thing," he says, noting the police who are everywhere: on horseback, on bicycles, walking the streets and manning the station on the corner of Seventh and Broadway. "It used to be that people were afraid to visit here, but now, everywhere you look you see parents with children and couples out on the town." He gestures to the hubbub of Times Square, with its lights and video screens.

"This used to be a prime pick-up area," Patrick says. Now it is filled with hotels, theaters, shops, restaurants and, most of all, tourists, despite the fact that it is nearly midnight. The sidewalks are jam-packed. There are street vendors, selling everything from pretzels to on-the-spot portraits. There are the down-and-outers playing their musical instruments or singing, with their hats on the ground at their feet, coins scattered around them. Occasionally, if the act is good, a crowd gathers to watch, although most are simply ignored as people push their way past. Here and there you see seedy-looking individuals with giant plastic garbage sacks, which they untie to reveal knock-offs of designer handbags or bootlegged videotapes and DVDs. What they are doing is illegal and they keep a close eye on the cops who stroll up and down the streets. The hustlers are always ready to quickly pack up and move along, but for the most part it's a pretty tame crowd.

"When I lived here people could find anything they wanted

in Times Square. Any kind of sex they wanted, any sort of sick thing anybody was into. The streets were lined with runaways, kids hooking or looking to score. They're still out here, the runaways and the homeless kids—kids in trouble. But the city, at least outwardly, has been cleaned up a lot."

He tells me about his first job in the city. Patrick first heard about Covenant International Foundation in New York from a news article he read in Chicago's O'Hare Airport in 1979, returning home to Bismarck from a stint as a counselor at a summer camp in Maine.

"The Savior of 42nd Street?" the headline said in bold, black print above a picture of a teenage runaway standing on a busy nighttime street corner in New York City. He saw the article again in a copy of a tabloid someone left on a seat at the gate where Patrick waited. The story was about runaways heading into what he would later learn was called The Minnesota Pipeline— kids leaving small towns and farms in the Midwest, looking for adventure in the big city. They were usually teenagers fed up with their parents or their homes for a variety of reasons—kids who hitched rides, rode buses or sometimes bought airline tickets to places like Minneapolis, Chicago, Los Angeles and New York, looking for fame, money and adventure. What they usually found instead was life-threatening trouble. There were predators on every corner, just waiting for lost kids to wander into their webs. The article gave a toll-free number, and Patrick wasted no time in calling it to offer his services. He had almost finished

at Minnesota State University-Moorhead, heading for a degree in social work, and needed an internship site. At first the New York program turned him down, saying he was too young, too small in size and too inexperienced. But he insisted and before he knew it, he had a job lined up in Hell's Kitchen, with Covenant International Foundation.

At first, the job was just what Patrick expected it to be. He lived in urban monastic housing with volunteers from around the country, working with runaways and street kids. His tasks were varied. On any given day he might help with lunch, route kids in or out of the shelter, steer them toward counselors or nearby clinics, or drive them to appointments or meetings with their probation officers. He never knew what he might be called on to do. That was part of what made the job exciting.

It wasn't unusual for him and a partner to venture out into the streets around the program's shelter, looking for kids who were in trouble or who needed a place to stay. He got to the point where he recognized many of the prostitutes and gang members who lined the streets around Hell's Kitchen. He helped them when they would accept help, and for the most part they treated him with respect. He never took his surroundings for granted, and he knew that the streets and alleys of New York could be deadly, but he had reached a point where he felt relatively comfortable stopping to talk with the prostitutes who worked the streets. He believed that this was the type of work he was called to do. But over time, the work lost some of its appeal. Despite his conviction that this was his vocation, he felt restless.

For one thing, he didn't really believe he was making much of a difference in the kids' lives. It seemed to him that the same ones moved in and out of the shelter week after week, using it almost as a hotel, a place where they could crash whenever they wanted to hang out with friends or when their own homes became inhospitable for whatever reason. These were often older, violent kids, most of them drug users, and it wasn't unusual for their primary caregivers, usually single mothers or grandmothers, to toss them out for days or weeks at a time. He rarely saw any real change in their lives, and the kids didn't seem to want change.

At the same time, his organizational skills and his knack for handling administrative tasks—those gifts that had served him so well leading the altar boys and Boy Scouts during his childhood—were catching the attention of Father Bruce Ritter, the founder and head of Covenant International Foundation. Within months, Patrick had been moved from volunteer to full-time employee, working in the main offices of Covenant International Foundation. It became Patrick's job to arrange Ritter's speaking tours, book his daily appointments, and make sure that he made it to fundraising events on time. He also got a first-hand look at how a major charity operated, how decisions were made, how finances were allocated. It was work that he was good at. He had a talent for remembering details, for keeping complicated schedules in his head, for understanding how big business worked. Even more significant, he now had the type of job that his father would appreciate and understand. He was on the fast track, just starting to climb a corporate ladder, and certain that if he wanted it, he could become a top executive in New York. He should have been on top of the world, and yet, something still didn't feel right. He still couldn't shake his growing restlessness.

It took a runaway from upstate New York to make him see that his life was not heading in the direction that God had planned for him, although he now sees those months in New York as a kind of classroom for what would come later. Patrick had entered Covenant International Foundation with a great amount of innocence and naïveté. What he had not expected was the big-business aspects of this charity. The idea was to raise money, and lots of it, using carefully orchestrated marketing techniques designed to hit donors where they lived. Granted, Patrick believed most of the money was being used to do God's work. Yet, the crass attitudes of some of those in the corporate hierarchy were eye opening for him. Still, he tried to see through the bureaucracy to the children who were helped.

One day, Patrick recalls being in his office trying to work out kinks in his boss's schedule when he heard one of the counselors talking about a boy he had just picked up downtown. It was a blond kid from upstate, somewhere around Rochester, who had arrived on the bus wearing a letterman's jacket and leather loafers. He apparently had no idea where he was going or what he would do when he got there. He was spotted wandering into one of New York's red light districts carrying a suitcase, and loaded down with cash and expensive electronic equipment.

"Luck must be with him," he heard Willard, another volunteer, say, "because some lady spotted him and insisted he call our number. Then she stayed with him until we got there. I just brought him in."

Curious, Patrick wandered down the hall to the recreation area and saw the boy surrounded by other kids. He was showing them the stuff in his suitcase, trying to impress and befriend them. Patrick could see them practically licking their chops as they took in the expensive leather of the boy's travel bag and the boy's fancy watch.

"Wow, he really is like a lamb to the slaughter. Did we call his parents yet?" Patrick asked Willard, still watching the scene in the rec room.

"Won't give his name," Willard replied. "But we're working on it."

"Maybe we should at least lock up some of his stuff," Patrick said before stepping into the rec room and approaching the circle of kids. He struck up a stilted conversation with the boy, who was basking in the attention of all his new, cool friends.

"Where're you from?" he asked.

"Upstate," the boy said, but would volunteer no more

information about himself. Patrick didn't work directly with the kids that much in his new position, but in this case he decided to do some checking on his own, to see if any runaways had been reported in some of the upstate counties. This kid wasn't run-of-the-mill.

"Stay put," he told the boy, "and I'll hang on to this for you," he said, scooping up the suitcase and snapping it shut.

"Hey!" the kid said, holding out his arm.

"Don't worry, you'll get it back. I'm locking it in the office for safe keeping," he answered, throwing a meaningful glance at the group of kids in the rec room. The blond boy didn't argue further. Instead, he turned back to continue his conversation with his new buddy, Chris.

Patrick found the boy's name on his luggage tag and an hour later, had determined that he had boarded a bus in Rochester. And though he had also found the phone number for his parents, there was no answer when he tried to call their number. He decided he'd talk with the boy, and then try the number again. If that didn't work, he'd contact the authorities in Rochester. When he returned to the rec room, though, it was deserted.

All Patrick could think about was this kid, green as grass, out there on the streets of New York having God knows what happening to him. He went out and searched high and low. Willard went with him. They hunted the streets until 2 a.m., without a trace, before finally heading back in for some sleep.

But, he had trouble sleeping.

In the year that he had been in New York, Patrick had seen kids do a lot of dumb and dangerous things, but this kid, out there alone, wouldn't stand a chance. He remembered his own first few hours in New York. During his first 60 minutes in the city a sleazy guy in a cheap, three-piece suit had offered to "get him into the movies." Had he been a little bit younger, a little bit more naïve, who knows what might have happened?

Looking for lost kids was not the job he had been hired to do, but he felt responsible for this one because he had walked away from him. He realized now what a mistake that had been, how attractive a rich, blond kid would look to some of the tough street kids who frequented the shelter. Sure, he had told him to stay where he was, but what had made him think the boy would listen? Really, the only thing he could do was to go back out and look again.

Patrick and Willard drove out a short time later in a car borrowed from the project. Willard had just arrived from his teaching job in the Bronx. He was more realistic than Patrick had been when he first arrived. His classroom had its share of tough kids, and he didn't expect as much from a shelter that catered to street-hardened young criminals. But he also realized that the kid he had brought in the day before was as good as dead if they didn't find him soon. He had agreed to take one more stroll down Eighth Avenue, through New York's toughest red light district, and after that they were calling the police.

"I should have stayed with him," Patrick said to Willard as he watched the street on either side. "I saw how the others were looking at him."

"You're being a little hard on yourself there, Pat. I mean, you could say the same thing about me. We both gave the kid credit for having some sense. You told him to stay put. I told him to stay put."

"Yeah, but this kid has a chauffer who drives him to school. Not exactly ready for reality, is he?"

They parked the car about a block from a dance club and got out. It was a very tough neighborhood. Drug deals were ignored and there were so many pimps and hookers that police mainly patrolled just to keep the tourist muggings down. Not that many tourists wandered into this neighborhood. Those who did were looking for a specific kind of encounter. Kids stood on every street corner, some of them boys and girls barely out of junior high, sidling out into the street every time the light changed.

They looked tough, but Patrick had talked with enough of them to know that beneath the streaked make-up and shaggy bangs were scared, homesick children. This was territory he had visited often during his first months in New York, looking for kids who had had enough and wanted to go home. One of the girls on the corner caught his attention.

"Hey, Patrick!"

It was Nicole, a girl from Wisconsin who had spent quite a

bit of time in the shelter. She was on a definite downward spiral and looked so sick that Patrick figured she'd be dead before long.

"Hey Nicki. How you holding up?"

"Good. Great." She had a bruise across the side of her face that makeup couldn't cover and she was clearly favoring one of her arms as if her shoulder were injured, but she was still out there hooking. She probably had no choice. "Can you spot me twenty until next week?"

"No money, Nicole. You know that. I'll buy you something to eat, though."

"Not hungry. But thanks. Catch you later, OK?" She started to wander off but Patrick called her back.

"Hey, we're looking for somebody. Blond kid, good haircut. Blue eyes, maybe wearing a letterman's jacket?"

"Oh, yeah, I saw him. A kid like that stands out. He was with some older guy who was shopping him around."

"When?"

"Earlier. He looked stoned."

"They were in Enrique's?" he said, indicating the dance club across the street.

"Yeah. Started out there."

"Thanks."

"No problem."

"Nicole, if … "

"Yeah, I know," she said, cutting him off. "See you around,

Patrick." With that she turned and walked back out into the street.

Patrick shook his head watching her, then turned back to Willard. "How much money have you got?"

"Why?"

"Cover. Looks like we're going to have to buy our way in."

They paid the cover charge for the strip joint and went inside. They lucked out. Right away they spotted the boy sitting with a seedy-looking character at a table in the back. He was awake, but just barely. His eyes were glassy and he looked sick.

"How do you want to play this?" Willard asked.

"Not alone, that's for sure. I'll go see if I can scare up a cop while you keep an eye on him, make sure he doesn't leave."

"What are we, Starsky and Hutch?" Willard asked, but his laugh had no humor in it. "I'll do my best, but don't be long," he called out to Patrick's retreating back.

He kept his distance for a while, but when it appeared that the man and boy were about to leave, Willard approached them, hoping to buy a little time. He didn't say anything at first, just sort of hovered, keeping his eye on the kid. It didn't take long for the older man to notice him and motion him over.

"You looking or buying?" he asked.

"Depends. How much for Joe Suburb here?" Willard asked, still peering at the kid with interest. The boy didn't even look up.

"Hundred bucks, 20 minutes."

"How about 50 bucks for ten minutes and we go out to my car?" As he said it, he noted with tremendous relief that two police officers were entering the club through the main door. They began scanning the crowd. The man who had been with the kid saw them at the same moment. He stood up.

"Tell you what, buddy," he said to Willard, "take him. Buy him a drink...call him a cab. Whatever. I've got appointments." With that he walked around the bar and through the back door of the club.

"Hey, kid," Willard said to the slouched figure in the corner of the booth. "This is your lucky day." The boy began to cry.

Patrick would never forget the look on that boy's face. The kid would be lucky if his short adventure in New York City didn't leave him with enough diseases to kill him. Regardless, it would likely take the boy a lifetime to forget the last two days. They finally reached his mother, who seemed more angry than concerned. They put him on the next bus back to Rochester.

Patrick would not be able to forget Nicki either, or the countless other wounded children who came through the shelter during his time in New York. There seemed so little he could really do for them. It was already too late for most. And how much could he do from behind a desk, writing administrative memos and scheduling appointments?

Searching for the purpose in what he was doing and not finding any answers, he began to look in new directions. As he read the daily newspaper, he found himself spending more time on the Help-Wanted ads, something he had never done before, and he hesitated over posters on the staff bulletin board that offered different volunteer and mission opportunities. Finally, frustrated at not feeling any clear direction from God, he borrowed a car and drove to rural Lancaster County in southern Pennsylvania, where he began a 10-day retreat. His bed was a mat on the floor of a bus that had been towed into the woods and outfitted with a wood-burning stove. His food was provided by the retreat center's host family, and consisted of grains and fruits. He took his daily baths from a pitcher of water that the host family carried out to him each morning. During long walks in the woods and almost angry talks with God, he asked what he was supposed to be doing next. He still talks about a night when he got into a shouting match with his creator.

"I remember hollering, 'Look, you're the one who gave me this stupid vocation. Don't tell me you meant for me to spend my life behind a desk in some New York charity's corporate office, so dammit, what am I supposed to do?' I must have looked like a lunatic, but this place was pretty remote, so I doubt anybody heard me. God did, of course," he says with a laugh.

Finally, free of distractions, he felt an answer forming in his head. Weeks earlier, while walking through the concrete jungles of midtown Manhatten, he had seen an advertisement for a volunteer to drive a tractor at an agricultural co-op for war widows in a small town in Guatemala, Central America. He hadn't paid much attention to it at the time. After all, he didn't know a word of Spanish, and while he did have a vague notion of where Guatemala was, he knew almost nothing about it. But for some reason, that advertisement kept popping into his head. It suddenly felt right to him. He was at peace with the idea in a way he hadn't been for a long time. He told himself it would be an adventure if nothing else, and if there was one thing he knew how to do, it was plow a straight row. Within days he had resigned from his corporate desk job and began to scour libraries and book stores, looking for anything he could find on Central America. He was Guatemala bound.

CHAPTER FIVE

An annual report

"El Norte"—the forested and mountainous northern section of Guatemala, is rich in a native culture that exists today very much as it has for the past several hundred years.

12-year-old Roberto came to us from "El Norte," the northeast. It was there that the violence of war brutally and quickly destroyed Roberto's heritage, killing his parents, brothers, and other relatives as his family worked their rocky farmland one summer evening. Roberto wandered from the charred ruins and joined dozens of likewise orphaned children who were housed and fed by a local minister until a telegram could be sent to the children's shelter.

"Too much has happened," Roberto told the shelter's executive director, Pat Atkinson, when he arrived, "and it hurts too much to talk about it." In fact, it was weeks before Roberto could begin to speak of his past. That is often the case with children of war..."

—Patrick Atkinson, Executive Director

The Dreamer Center
SAN FELIPE SLUMS, ANTIGUA, GUATEMALA
Nov. 1, 2000

Carlitos' story is like so many others that Atkinson has either heard, or been involved in, since his arrival in Central America in 1983.

"Can it really have been 17 years ago?" he wonders aloud. And yet, when he thinks of all the faces of the children who have passed through his life, all of the weddings, christenings and funerals he has attended, it makes sense. Some he has adopted, either formally or informally. Others he has simply taken under his wing. All are like family to him. They call him Papito. He never met Carlitos until the morning he stumbled over him at his door. And yet, Patrick drops an entire day's work and gives Carlitos' problem his full attention.

"Now begins one of the most challenging parts of the job of getting medical help for this kid," he says, picking up the phone again. He calls Sonia Xinico, a child he pulled from a burning village when he first arrived in Guatemala. She is nearly finished studying for her law degree and does much of the legal work for the mothers and children in the project.

"Sonia," Patrick says, "We have a kid here who needs help." He quickly relates Carlitos' story, and asks her to begin the legal work that will be necessary if he is to take the little boy out of the country. It is never easy. These children frequently don't have birth certificates—since many are born at home. And because he's an orphan, it will be doubly tough. The government is always concerned that children will be spirited out and not returned. That would be a particular worry in this case, because Carlitos is a witness, perhaps the only witness, in a capital murder trial.

"It could take a while," Sonia warns Patrick.

"Do your best," he says. "I really don't know how much time this kid has." As he hangs up, he leans back in his chair and says, "Sonia is one of our success stories. When I look at her, I know that this has all been worth it."

"Was she a street child?" I ask.

"No, she was a child of war." He closes his eyes. He doesn't like to talk about the day he first met Sonia or think about the war years, but he says if I'm going to tell his story, I need to understand what those early days were like. Later that night, he tells me about the wars he's seen, and as he talks, I realize for the first time what Patrick tries so hard to hide—that he is frequently afraid.

Chimaltenango
GUATEMALA, CENTRAL AMERICA
April 1984

The soldier pointed his automatic rifle through the passenger-side window at Patrick's face.

"Tell your driver to turn the car around," he said with

authority. "This road is closed."

"Perhaps there's a toll?" Edgar Cabnal, Patrick's assistant, asked from the driver's seat. He reached into his pocket, preparing to offer a bribe, but saw the soldier's finger tighten on the trigger.

"OK! OK!" Edgar raised his hands in a signal of surrender and shifted the car into reverse.

"Must have been some battle," he murmured to Patrick, who could only manage a nod until they had rounded a curve and the soldiers were no longer visible. Patrick took a deep breath, and could feel the nervous sweat dripping down between his shoulder blades. The back of their Toyota Land Rover was filled with medical supplies. Had the soldiers decided to take a look, those supplies would have been reason enough to kill them. The fact that they were intended for women and children would have meant nothing. The soldiers would have assumed they were intended for the rebels hiding in the mountains. The truth was no shield against violence in this place. Patrick glanced down at the telegram he still held in his lap.

"Big battle. Many dead. Please come." That was all it said. Such telegrams were not unusual. The Indian village in Chimaltenango was in the middle of the war zone. It was mountainous, which meant that the rebels hiding in the passes above often walked through its dirt-packed streets in search of provisions. The people who lived in the village were powerless to keep them out, but even if the rebels simply took the food without asking, as they often did, the soldiers saw this as aiding the enemy and would sometimes punish the entire town— usually by shooting the men, and sometimes killing or raping the women and children as well. Patrick wasn't sure what had happened during this particular battle, but the army clearly didn't want any outsiders to know about it. As an outsider, he had no business being there as far as the soldiers were concerned.

"So now," Patrick asked Edgar. "What do we do?"

"We go around," he replied. Edgar was second in command at the orphanage that Patrick directed in Antigua, but here, he was the expert. These hills were his home and he knew them well. "I can get us there. It's just going to take us half the day. Oh, well," he continued as he swung the Land Rover off the road and onto a track through the trees, "nobody ever said social work would be easy."

Edgar was actually in more danger than Patrick. As a Guatemalan, if he were caught disobeying the soldier's orders, he would probably be beaten, shot and would disappear, as was happening to thousands of others who were getting caught in the middle of Guatemala's most recent civil war. This fighting, which had begun in 1960 and would continue for 36 years, had started under the guise of stopping the spread of communism across the small Central American countries. Actually, though, it was based on fear and greed. Large tracts of undeeded land that had been owned for centuries by Guatemala's Mayan Indian tribes were wanted by the country's rich and powerful for planting coffee and other agricultural export crops. Under the soil were also vast oil reserves that flowed into Southern Mexico. Where the Mayan Indians had for generations traded and recorded land ownership by honor and word-of-mouth, the newer, more urban national leadership now insisted that ownership be proven by nonexistent paper contracts and recorded land titles. Land grabs of unrecorded property led to violence, massacres led to revenge, and the cycle of violence, once started, mushroomed into a war that would divide the country for three generations. As is always the case with war, the big losers were the innocent women and children.

As Patrick and Edgar rounded the corner of an old riverbed there was an unmistakable stench of a body left to rot among the trees. Patrick could see the naked corpse tied to a stump. He couldn't tell if it was a man or a woman, but whoever it was had obviously been murdered. They didn't stop.

It was nearly midday before they reached the outskirts of the village. They could smell the smoke for miles before they actually turned onto the main road into town. The smoke hovered over the deserted street, and an unnatural quiet hung over the small village. Normally, at this time of day, the paths and courtyards would be filled with women tending to their cooking fires, their children getting underfoot as they moved from table to fire pit and back again. The men should have been standing around chatting to one another over cornstalk fences, sharing news of the day or cleaning their farming tools. On this afternoon, though, there was nobody. The only sound was that of a baby crying in the distance. The telegram had come from the village priest, so Patrick's first thought was to find the church. Edgar stopped in front of what appeared to be the town's main building on one side of the public square. This was where the smoke originated. The flames were out, but the embers were still smoldering. While the shell of the building still stood, the interior was gutted and the windows and doorways were blackened with soot. Patrick climbed out of the Landrover and slowly approached the window. The heat had cooled enough so that he could lean his head inside, but he immediately wished he hadn't. He could see charred remains of bodies piled together. He turned back to Edgar. For a moment he couldn't speak. He felt sick. He swallowed hard several times and finally managed to say, "Let's find whoever's in charge."

They drove to the other side of the courtyard to the wooden church, distinguishable from the other buildings by a cross on the roof. They knocked, but there was no answer.

"It's pretty clear that the men are gone, but where are the women and kids?" Patrick wondered.

"Hiding," Edgar replied. "They don't know who we are, and I'm guessing they aren't taking any chances. That crying is coming from over there," Edgar said, indicating a cornfield on the opposite end of the village. "They're hunkered down. Let's unload this stuff at least. They'll need the medicine and blankets."

As they worked, stacking boxes on the street in front of the church, an old woman suddenly peered out from the doorway of a nearby hut. She held her arms tightly against her chest, rocking back and forth from one foot to another as she stood watching them. Finally, a low wail started from somewhere deep in her chest, shattering the silence. Tears flowed down her face.

"My sons!" she cried in broken Spanish. She seemed to be addressing Edgar and Patrick, so Patrick stopped what he was doing and approached her. "My sons!" she said again, pointing to the burned-out building. Behind her, Patrick could see a child peeking out. It was a little girl, perhaps six or seven, holding tightly to the old woman's skirts.

The little girl cried silently, wadding the material from her grandmother's dress into her fist, and stuffing the fabric into her mouth. Her dirty face was awash with hours' worth of tears. The woman reached around and grabbed the little girl, thrusting her toward Patrick and Edgar. The child turned around and clung.

"No!" the little girl screamed, terrified, but the old woman didn't listen.

"Take her," she insisted. "Take her away, it's too dangerous here. Save her—my son's child. Take her!" she cried.

Patrick shook his head and began backing away.

"No. I brought medicine and supplies. Here, it's all here," he said, indicating the pile on the ground behind him.

"Take her!" She said again, prying the child's hands from

her arms and shoving her at Patrick a second time.

"I can't," he said a little desperately, and climbed back into the vehicle, closing the door. "Edgar, let's go!" But as they tried to drive away, the old woman stood in front of the car, and they were forced to stop. She ran around to the side and pushed the sobbing and kicking child through the window right into Patrick's lap.

Before he could push her back out again other women appeared from other houses, running forward, shoving other children at him or lifting them into the back of the Land Rover. They ranged in age from two to eight or nine. All of them were screaming and crying in the Cackchiquel Indian dialect that Patrick barely understood. As quickly as they had come, the women stepped back and began to pray in their Mayan language, leaving their 14 shell-shocked, terror-stricken kids.

"What do you want to do?" Edgar yelled over the din.

"Well, we can't hang around here. If those soldiers find us, we're toast. Let's take them with us for now, and we can sort it out later. We can take them back to the orphanage." As they drove away, the children reached their arms out of the Land Rover, calling back to their mothers and grandmothers, pleading, screaming and crying. They never stopped. Five minutes down the road, Patrick also heard the sounds of vomiting in the back. The reek of unwashed bodies mingled with the stench of sickness as the vehicle picked its way slowly through the forest. The trip into the village had taken hours, and so did the trip out. The crying continued, a little more quietly. It was heartbreaking to hear. Eventually the two men and the children reached a main road and their pace picked up.

"I suppose they're hungry," Edgar said as they left the hill country behind and headed into the outskirts of Antigua. "I know I am," he added.

Patrick wasn't sure he would ever want to eat again after what he'd seen that day, but he knew it had been many hours since most of the children had even had a drink. Sick as they'd been, he knew they must be thirsty.

"Let's pull in up here," he said, indicating a roadside café about a half hour from Antigua. As the children piled out of the Land Rover, Patrick realized he couldn't take them inside. Not only had they been sick, many were so scared that they'd wet themselves. He pointed out a row of tables under some nearby trees, and Edgar led the children to it. For the moment, the weeping had let up as they took in their new surroundings.

When Patrick returned with 14 hamburgers, orders of fries and Cokes, most of the children accepted the food suspiciously. They gulped down the drinks, but pried apart the burgers for a closer look.

"They don't know what to do with it, do they?" Patrick commented as one little boy attempted to flatten the bun.

"No...these kids eat beans, corn, rice and tortillas," said Edgar. "See, he's probably trying to make a tortilla out of it." The others were doing the same. Miserable as they were, Patrick knew it would not occur to a hungry Guatemalan child to turn down food when it was offered. But once they were back on the road, it didn't take the men long to realize their mistake as the vomiting started again. And then the crying started again too.

"Now what?" Patrick wondered aloud.

"Let's sing," Edgar suggested.

"Sing?"

"Yeah. Kid songs. You know any?"

"I don't know any kids songs in Spanish," he replied.

"That's OK, Pat. Most of these kid don't speak Spanish."

"True," he said sheepishly. "OK, here goes," he said, relying heavily on his old camp counselor skills. In as loud a voice as he could manage, he belted out the words to *Old McDonald*. It worked. Silence descended on the truck as the children quieted to listen. He sang it again, and then again. He was still singing when they rolled up to the door of the orphanage an hour later.

Finding room for more children was always a problem. Patrick, as executive director of one of Guatemala's largest orphanages, was always receiving children at the door. But 14 at one time was a particular challenge. He gathered cushions and spread them on the floor, found enough blankets, toothbrushes and clean clothes to go around, had staff run everybody through the shower and begin the long process of de-lousing. Then, he sat with them through that first long night.

The child who touched Patrick's heart the most was the little girl whom he had first seen hiding behind her grandmother's skirts. He found a friend of a friend to interpret her words as she explained what had happened to her home and family. Through her tears, she told him that her father had been a leader among the men in the village. She referred to him as the mayor. She said he had called a meeting of the men because he had wanted to buy medicine for her, to help heal her stomach. She said she got bad stomachaches that her father said were caused by worms. He didn't have enough money for the medicine, but she had heard him tell her grandmother that if all of the families with sick kids put their money together they could buy a lot of the medicine, at a better price. The men had been meeting to discuss the idea when the soldiers drove into town. The child said there had been a lot of yelling and angry words. She had heard the word "Communist." That's what one of the soldiers kept calling her father as he hit him. It didn't help that the rebels had been through the village the night before, demanding food at gunpoint. The villagers had little choice but to give it to them, but the soldiers didn't listen to explanations.

All of the women and children ran away, and they didn't see the soldiers set fire to the building where the men had been meeting, but they heard the screams and the gunfire. The rest of the little girl's family had scattered, her brothers into the hills, her mother and sisters into hiding. Not sure what to do next, she had crept home to her grandmother's house, taking the long way around to avoid the burning building.

She didn't know who in her family was alive, or who was

dead. She had found many of the missing on the floor of the burned-out church, where they had been stacked like cordwood.

Patrick could do little to heal her past, except hold her and the other children when they cried and see to it that they were well cared for inside the orphanage. As the weeks went by, he did what he could to help guarantee their futures. Those who were old enough were enrolled in school, and he started encouraging them to dream of something better. In the weeks that followed these massacres, he also tried to return some of the children to their relatives in the village, and did his best to identify all of them. But many of the mothers were forced to go into the city to try to find work and their whereabouts were unknown. Others simply didn't want to be found. They felt that their children were better off in the orphanage, where at least they were fed regularly and didn't have to hide from men with guns.

For too long, fear had been a way of life in Guatemala's mountains.

Patrick remembers his first impressions of Guatemala when he had arrived months earlier—a land rich in beauty and tradition, but whose people were among the poorest in the world.

"I never did drive that tractor on the farm for war widows," he says with a shake of his head. By the time he arrived, he explains, plans for the farm had fallen through and the land had been abandoned in the wake of the endless fighting between the American-backed government soldiers and the indigenous rebel guerillas.

Besides, his talent for organization had been recognized as just the thing that the orphaned children in the villages surrounding Antigua needed. The Covenant International Foundation orphanage outside Antigua was in desperate need of a director, and Patrick was asked to hold that job until someone else could be found to take it over. Although he spoke no Spanish and didn't want to go back into administration, he agreed, "But only for six months," he told them, "and then I'm going home."

The villages in Chimaltenango weren't the first he had been to. The misfortunes that had befallen the people there were common. Many times in the months following his arrival, he had been forced to abandon his car at the side of the road and escape into the brush rather than face oncoming patrols or risk getting caught in gunfire between warring factions.

Once he had stumbled right into the middle of a battle and had found himself surrounded by corpses—people cut down by machine gun fire. There had been little time to react. Bullets were still whizzing around him. Without thinking, he had reached down and wiggled a crying baby out from under a dead woman. He had run with the naked infant back to his Land Rover and drove away, still holding the child on his lap. He had named the boy Francisco in remembrance of St. Francis of Assisi's prayer to make us instruments of peace, but he never did find out who the child's parents were.

Another time, while delivering blankets and medicine to an impoverished village in El Salvador, he saw bodies floating in a meandering river. Spotting a group of crying women, he stopped to help. He picked up a badly injured child, not even realizing at first that he held the little boy's torso in one arm, his severed leg in the other. That child died moments later.

He has rocked children who were dying of burns they got from phosphorous bombs dropped from low-flying airplanes. He has seen children shot for no apparent reason while they played soccer in abandoned fields. Sometimes, when the age was right, he knew the boys could be conscripted into the army at the point of a gun—kids herded into the backs of trucks and driven away by groups of soldiers, frequently never seeing their families again.

He still thinks about Maximo, a little boy who had escaped death twice, but who would live with the emotional scars forever.

"One night, in the wee hours of the morning, Maximo wandered into my office and sat down at my feet," Patrick says. "I smiled, then pretended to continue working. I knew he had something he needed to say, and after a while, he started talking. Whenever I looked at him, he stopped. So long as I didn't look up and pretended to work, Maximo's story poured out of him."

The boy explained that the people of his village had built an underground cellar and had learned to hide in it whenever strangers approached—soldiers, guerillas, anybody unfamiliar. Whoever wandered through the area would find a deserted village. It worked well for a long time, but somebody finally tipped off the army. One day, soldiers drove into the apparently abandoned town, brought out dogs and within minutes, found the hiding place. Then they tossed a grenade inside the cellar and waited. Nearly everybody died that day—his mother, his sisters and brothers, his cousins and grandmother. Not Maximo, though, because he and his grandfather had gone to the river to fish. They were caught unaware on their return trip and soldiers tied them both to a tree. Maximo was forced to watch as his grandfather was tortured. They beat him with sticks and cut his tongue out before finally finishing him off with a knife to the throat. For some reason they didn't kill the little boy, though. They simply walked away, leaving him tied to that tree. He was discovered three days later by someone walking along the remote path. By then he was nearly dead.

He whispered to Patrick that he wished he *had* died that day, along with the rest of his family. The stranger who found him had left him at the door of Patrick's orphanage. Maximo wasn't grateful.

"What frightened me most about Maximo at the time was that he had not cried," Patrick says. "Not once since he arrived. He spoke in whispers, and told his story in a detached sort of way, almost as if he were relating an event that had happened to someone else."

Patrick understood that feeling. By then he had heard too many stories like Maximo's in the two years he had been in

Guatemala. He had seen too much pain, had held too many dying kids. He was becoming numb, too. He had learned to put one foot in front of the other and do what needed to be done, without letting it touch his heart. But he couldn't control his nightmares any more than Maximo could. He walked the boy back to bed and tucked him in, ruffled his hair and started to leave.

"Leave the light on," the little boy whispered.

Patrick understood. There were things he shared with that little boy that his friends and family in North Dakota could never understand.

"You know how soldiers don't want to talk about their war experiences when they return? I understand that perfectly," he tells me over dinner, and yet, it bothers him that the people he is closest to know so little about those years of his life.

He relates a conversation that he overhead one night at a family gathering, about the military draft in America. His mother said she had always been grateful that her children had reached adulthood at a time when there was no draft—that all of them had managed to escape the horrors of war.

"It was at that point," he says, "that I realized they had no idea what my life has been like. I spent years in a war zone, basically helpless, doing things that were sometimes stupid, frequently very dangerous. I spent years scared to death or horrified by the images I was seeing, and yet, I couldn't talk about them. But they were wrong. They definitely had one son who went to war. He's still there."

He speaks with anger about the "so-called activitists who spent the war years in Seattle or drinking tea on Long Island," who then criticized him for not doing more to stop human rights violations in Guatemala.

"One person wrote, 'Patrick Atkinson fished bodies out of the river downstream. Why didn't he wade upstream and stop the ones who were throwing the bodies into the water in the first place?' I'll bet that was easy for someone to write from their beautiful backyard in the United States. I was in the war zone trying to help. Where were *they* while the war was being fought?" He takes a deep breath, lets it out slowly, and smiles ruefully. "Sorry," he says, "but this subject always upsets me." He pays the bill and we leave. It is a lovely night, clear and crisp and very dark. There are no modern streetlights to block out the evening's stars. We walk in silence to Patrick's car and return to the office. I worry that I've upset him, but he's already moved on to something else.

"I need to call a judge who happens to be a friend of mine and see if I can't expedite the paperwork for Carlitos," he says. "I can't save the country, but maybe we can save this one little kid."

CHAPTER SIX

Patrick Atkinson's Last Will and Testament

Dear Family and Friends,

Being a practical person and knowing the possible health risks that I may encounter as I travel alone for the next several months, I have also seen to complete my business and update my will in Bismarck.

This letter is a continuance of the process of preparing for the eventuality of my death. The goal is to offer assistance in the difficult decisions that surface at a time such as this.

To this end:

If I should disappear, then you should know that there is a recent portrait on file at Photo Express in Bismarck   Dr. Dean Knutsen has my dental X-rays.

I do not approve of paying ransom for kidnap victims under any circumstances, as I believe that it only encourages this inhumane practice. We cannot hold ourselves responsible for that which others do to us, but rather only for that which we do to others.

Under no circumstances do I want anybody to engage in extraordinary and mechanical methods to sustain life where a reasonable recovery is not expected. Death is not the termination of life; rather, it is a passage to that which is much better. It is also the means through which we unite ourselves with our God and join Him in the very same peace that I have worked so hard for these past several years. I don't fear death in the least and readily recognize its inevitability for us all.

If I should die overseas and my body is found, then my first preference is that any and all usable organs, etc. be removed and taken advantage of to their fullest. My body was a loaner, and I can think of no finer gift than to pass it to somebody else who can use it once my spirit has been released.

I would not mind in the least being cremated and having my ashes disposed of in a suitable manner. In my dreams I would have the ashes spread on the Missouri River where I spent so many of my younger years and enjoyed life to its fullest. It was always so beautiful there, there was so much to discover and so many fantasies of freedom that came true there throughout the years. Some of my fondest memories from my earliest to my last years in life are of this grand river. I have checked and this would be acceptable to both the Catholic Church and the city of Bismarck.

If you would rather not cremate me, and I would readily understand that, then I would like to be buried in Bismarck. I always loved Bismarck and planned to move back there one day.

I would ask that the funeral be kept as inexpensive as possible. I tried to live for the poor and gave away much of what I had, and would feel rather silly if thousands were spent on a fancy casket that will be visible for only a day or two. Please keep everything inexpensive and have the rest go to help any foundations and scholarships that I may establish in my will.

If I should die overseas and my body is not found, then you should not worry. The body was simply God's gift with which I was able to accomplish much in a short period of time. It was, after all, never that good looking and was too short, but it worked hard, took a lot of abuse and kept the spirit warm while it finished whatever work it could.

Besides this, you should each know and remember always of my love and appreciation for your presence in my life, and I eagerly await being able to hug, dance, boat and rejoice with you again in some future time.

With much love, and in His name,
Patrick Atkinson

When Patrick tells his stories, people sometimes react with disbelief. He has been called the Indiana Jones of Good Works, because it's difficult to fathom that so much has happened to one man. The result is that he doesn't talk about his past to very many people anymore. He has a few stock stories that he trots out for reporters. His near-death experience explains why he is willing to wade into dangerous situations, and why it seems he's given up any semblance of a normal life to do what very often is a thankless job. He talks about one or two of the massacres he's witnessed because they are so dramatic, and illustrate how desperate the times have sometimes been in places like Guatemala and El Salvador. He will also tell people, if pressed, about the time he was tossed from bed by a bomb blast in El Salvador, or about how he smuggled money into Panama. What he doesn't say, is how frightening these experiences were, how they made him long for a quiet life by the Missouri River. When he talks to audiences about the children he rescues, he doesn't mention the price he's paid—how he never has a serious girlfriend anymore because it's too emotionally dangerous to get close to anybody, only to have them leave. Or about how, during his frequent travels, he often wakes up alone in the dark, listening to the midnight sounds for some clue as to where he might be in the world. He doesn't talk about his bouts of depression, his anger, his feelings of helplessness in the face of so much need—feelings which he battles alone and in silence, cutting himself off from friends until he finds his equilibrium again. These are decisions he made a long time ago, while he was traveling from one violent Central American country to the next.

"People don't want to hear how tired I am," he says. "They want to hear what it's like to be in a hotel that's bombed. Now THAT'S interesting."

I admit that I also want to hear those stories. He sighs and begins to recount the tales he's told so many times.

PORT AU PRINCE, HAITI
1986

Patrick had been staring at the same typed page for hours. He was sitting in the teeming airport terminal in Haiti's capital city just a few days after strongman dictator, "Baby Doc" Duvalier, had fled to France. He was trying to get a ride into his city center hotel, and while he waited, he was also trying to write a report on his progress in setting up new programs for street kids in the war-torn Latin American countries he had recently visited. Here, though, he was running into roadblocks, not the least of which was the war itself. It was preventing him from even leaving the smoke-filled Haitian airport terminal. Normally, he would have taken a bus into the capital, but there weren't any buses running. Planes were delayed by hours, sometimes days, and right now there didn't seem to be any people manning the desks at the airport, although the terminal itself was jam-packed with people. He packed up his equipment and wandered outside again to try to get a ride.

After an hour standing at the curb, he managed to flag down a battered cab, and when the driver got out to talk to him, he found out what was going on.

"Rioters," the taxi driver said. "The army is cracking down and there are road blocks. There are people missing. There are people resisting. See the fires?" he added, pointing to thick, black smoke rising over the distant city skyline.

"That looks like it's coming from downtown," Patrick replied.

"It is. Tires burning, I think. But whatever it is, we don't want any part of it. Many people have been killed," the driver said. He began to walk away. "You can't go in now. It's too dangerous."

"Look, I'm only going to be here for another 24 hours, and I have about a week's worth of work to do. What would it take for you to get me into the city center?" Patrick asked the retreating driver. "I'll find my own way around from there."

Turning back toward him, the taxi driver raised his hand and poked his index finger into Patrick's chest. "You want to go? (poke, poke) You sure you want to go?" he asked, poking yet again. "I'll take you, but it's going to cost you…one hundred dollars."

Patrick knew from past experience that the trip downtown should have cost about one dollar on the bus or eight dollars for a taxi ride. Still, as he looked at the long lines and the many bored faces at the airport, he knew he was in no position to bargain. "I'll take it," he said. "Let's go now."

Leaving the terminal, the driver turned off from the main highway and onto a back road that took them out into the countryside for a mile or so, heading away from the airport. "We'll go this way and get you to your hotel by the back streets."

But, as they crested a hill, they found themselves in the middle of an angry, chanting mob that stood clustered around a plywood speaker's platform where one man was giving what appeared to be a rallying speech. When the crowd saw the taxi, however, they stopped listening to the man, and instead, surrounded the car and began hitting it with their sticks and protest signs.

"Oh, God," Patrick said. "This is not good."

"You are a reporter," the driver said as he threw the car into park and opened his door.

"I'm not a reporter!" Patrick shouted back in confusion.

The driver pointed at the camera bag that Patrick had brought along with him, and which now sat on the seat beside him. "*Be* a reporter!" he said, before jumping out. He yelled, "I have a reporter here! He is from a big American magazine, and he is here to shoot pictures of you."

The crowd continued to shout and jump up and down. A few young children came up to the window of the taxi and watched through the glass as Patrick attached a telephoto lens to the Minolta that he normally used to provide illustrations for his reports. "This is not good," he said again, "this is definitely not good." He kept muttering it over and over to himself, fumbling with a camera lens that suddenly didn't seem to want to fit.

The driver stuck his head back into the open window of the car. "Get out now and start taking pictures!" he ordered. "A photographer knows how to work his camera." And so Patrick did.

The people surrounding the car picked up their signs again and waved them over their heads, yelling anti-government messages as Patrick clicked off frame after frame, using a camera that contained no film. He was still clicking away when the taxi driver shouted to the crowd, "The famous reporter has to go now," and then to Patrick he said, "Get back in the car!" Together, they got back into the taxi and pulled away, first driving around and then over burning trash that lay across the road as they continued into the heart of the city.

The rioting continued off and on in Port Au Prince for the next 24 hours as Patrick dashed from place to place in the city, visiting clinics and human rights centers, looking at abandoned schools and hospitals, and asking the prices of vacant lots. On one occasion he had to duck through a broken restaurant window when a group of rioters came running down the street, followed by a military truck carrying a mounted machine gun. From the back of the truck, a Haitian soldier was firing at the fleeing crowd. More than once, he saw a rioter go down in the street and lie still as other rioters jumped over or ran around the body.

Patrick saw the difficulties in establishing a good, stable shelter in Haiti, but he also saw the overwhelming need.

SAN SALVADOR, EL SALVADOR
1987

Around every corner in San Salvador and in nearly every doorway, Patrick ran across ragged, barefoot street children begging with outstretched hands. They quickly picked Patrick out as a foreigner and followed him. He felt like the Pied Piper, and on some days he had a hard time shaking them off. After he emptied his pockets of change, they still dogged his steps, speaking to him in their few phrases of English.

"You buy?" asked one little girl who was particularly persistent. She kept grabbing at his sleeve. He had given her several coins already, which she quickly pocketed, but still she refused to go away. She reached up again as he tried to talk with the owner of a building that had a "For Rent" sign on the front. Hearing him, she realized he could speak Spanish and she began an all-out verbal attack.

"Look, Señor, at this nice necklace for your wife, for your kid," she said, holding up a grubby, yet complicated piece of knotted string. Patrick said goodbye to the building owner, then beckoned for the little girl to follow him.

The look on her face suddenly changed from eager to wary. "Where?" she asked. She had learned early that there was more safety on the street. At least in the open, if she were threatened, somebody might come to her aid. The last thing she wanted to do was follow a stranger into a back alley.

But she trailed him at a distance as he walked up to a food vendor and handed him some paper money. "Feed this kid," he said, indicating the girl. She moved closer. "What do you want?" the vendor asked her. She pointed. Patrick stayed long enough to make certain she received the food before he left her standing there, wolfing down the beans and tortillas.

Later, in his report, he would write, "The need for a homeless shelter in San Salvador is tremendous. Many of these children have lost one or both parents to the war; most have no fathers to support them; and even when there is a mother at home, she frequently leaves the children for hours, days, even weeks at a time as she moves about in search of work. Prostitution is rampant; and when AIDS becomes more prevalent here, it is going to be devastating."

He put a hand on his stomach. He was finding it difficult to think about anything except the growing pain in his belly. It seemed worse tonight. He had lost at least 10 pounds in the last month. Nothing he ate stayed with him for very long. He figured it was either tapeworms or amoebas. Since his arrival in Central America five years earlier, he had been plagued by both, along with a host of other tropical ailments.

He tried to focus on his report once again. He would have to fly to the States to explain the shelter problems in person. As in Haiti, to open a shelter in El Salvador was possible, but it would take more money than he had been allocated. Finally, he closed the cover on his portable typewriter and stood up to stretch. He was so tired that his eyes burned from sweat and fatigue. Strolling out onto his hotel room's small, one-chair balcony, he stared up at the beautiful volcano that loomed in the distance, and thought about what he would be doing if he were back in the States. He climbed into bed, rolled onto his side, and despite feeling sick, nodded off almost instantly.

He was jarred awake sometime later that night by what felt like an intense, screaming pressure that blew him out of bed and against a nearby wall. The deafening roar that accompanied it shook the ground and shattered the glass in the window just above where he slept, jarring his head and clicking his teeth together hard.

He had been dreaming, and his first confused thought was that a drunk had broken into his room, grabbed his bed and flipped it up, throwing Patrick against the wall. But there was no drunk in the room, and there was nothing moving, only the sound of raining plaster and debris outside his hotel room, and sirens blaring in discord all around him. Then he heard shouts, the slap of running feet, more sirens, and crying. Patrick did a mental check for physical injuries as he hauled himself up from the floor—a few nicks from the flying glass, a chipped tooth, and one shard stuck into the back of his hand, which he plucked out without really considering what he was doing. The cut wasn't deep. He did have some pain in his leg and a nasty bruise developing just above his left knee—he must have smacked into something when he was thrown from the bed—but since the leg seemed to be working all right, he limped over to the window. He smelled burning gasoline from the street below and saw thick, black smoke coming from the street.

He stepped gingerly around the glass and through the shattered door that led onto his balcony, where he bent over the side to take a better look. "If that was a car bomb, it must have gone off right in front of the hotel," Patrick speculated. Ambulances, police cars, and military vehicles were filling up the street below. Leaving his hotel room, he walked to the glass-strewn lobby. The outer wall had been blown off the building across the street, and he could see into some of the ground floor rooms of that building through gaping holes. He was thankful he had not been in a ground floor room. Somehow he had lucked out, he thought. He was told by security staff to return to his room, so he did. Stepping through the room's broken sliding-glass door, he shook the glass off the balcony chair and sat down.

He supposed that he should probably leave the hotel to avoid the threat of fire, but he didn't. Now that the blast was over, it seemed to him that there was no reason to leave. The hotel alarms were no longer sounding and no one was telling him to get out. Besides, where would he go? It was the middle of the night, glass splinters lay scattered among his clothes and his papers, and he didn't like the idea of wandering alone in the streets of San Salvador in the middle of the night.

Going back into his room, he fiddled with the door on his mini fridge and grabbed a bottle. It was warm, but wet. He used the bottle opener attached to the wall before carrying the bottle out to the balcony. Sitting down again, he leaned far back in the seat and rested his feet over the railing. What should he do now, he wondered? Pray? Laugh? Cry? He couldn't seem to decide. So much for getting a nice, safe, good night's sleep, he thought.

Moments later he heard a high-pitched, whistling noise from behind him that turned out to be the screeching of El Salvadoran fighter jets flying low overhead. It seemed to Patrick as if he could reach up and touch them. Just as he saw the red lights of their afterburners overhead, they veered up and shot balls of fire into the side of the volcano that lay not more than a few miles in front of him. Explosions followed, throwing fiery debris high into the air. More fighter jets flew in, one after another dropping its payload on the beautiful volcanic mountainside. Before long there were dozens of small fires burning in the treetops over what must have been an entrenched rebel base. The army wasn't wasting any time in retaliating, he noted.

He felt like a spectator at a fireworks display, except that this time the results were horrific. He went back to the small refrigerator and grabbed another bottle.

Morning found him fast asleep in his chair, his feet still propped up on the railing. When he finally awoke, he added to his list of ailments a stiff neck, along with the injuries he had suffered the night before. He shook the remaining glass from his belongings, packed his bags and headed out to the street to get a taxi to the airport.

"And then there are the times I smuggled thousands of dollars into Panama," he says over dinner in his house later that night. It's noisy here. Patrick's son, Neto, has friends in and they're sitting around the living room eating pizza and watching a video. Patrick's home has always been a safe place for teens to congregate, and Friday night is a favorite time to do it. We are in his office down the hall. His computer screen is blinking and his instant-message alarm beeps frequently, but he seems able to concentrate on many things at once—answering his e-mails, eating pizza, and recounting yet another story of past danger.

"You smuggled money? Why? How?" I ask, momentarily forgetting my pizza.

"Why? Because my boss told me to. I don't think he fully understood the danger of it. As for how, I taped cash to my body."

The first time Patrick smuggled a large amount of cash into Panama, he did it in order to save a fledgling community development program that he had started there. It was during the reign of Panamanian strongman, Manuel Noriega. The U.S. government had placed a trade embargo on the Central American country, which meant American banks weren't allowed to wire money into Panama. Without an influx of U.S. cash, Patrick's Panamanian staff was not being paid, and food and medicines could not be bought.

"What I was doing was not illegal," he explains, "just dangerous. I always declared the money when I left the states. The government's issue wasn't in money going into Panama. They just didn't want it to go through Noriega's Central Bank. The trouble was, if the wrong people knew I had it, my chances of ending up dead in some field outside Panama City were astronomical. That kind of cash was an absolute fortune to those people."

Patrick would travel from Guatemala to Florida to pick up a prepared package of as much as $50,000 in U.S. $100 bills.

Careful to declare to Customs that he was carrying the cash so he wouldn't be arrested as a drug or arms dealer if searched, he kept the currency in his backpack until he was on board his next flight to Panama City. That part was easy. The trick was to get the money safely past the Panamanian customs agents and suspicious onlookers on the other end. Once airborne, he would slip into the airplane's bathroom, strip off his clothes and carefully wrap the money in small plastic bags, which he strapped to his body using surgical tape. Up and down and between his legs, across his chest, under his arms—he taped the tens of thousands of dollars in U.S. currency. The process always made him very nervous and by the time he was through he was always drenched in sweat.

Patrick worried about the sound of the tape as he unrolled it. He frequently stopped to listen for footsteps or voices outside the door. When he finished, he would wipe the sweat from his face, open the door and return to his seat, being careful to keep his facial expression neutral. He knew he couldn't appear nervous. It might draw unwanted attention.

When he took his seat and re-stowed his carry-on bag, he always felt as though a dozen pairs of eyes were on him. What, under normal circumstances, would have seemed to be a planeload of happy families returning home from a holiday, would begin to feel vaguely threatening.

Nor could he relax when the plane touched down in Panama City. If anything, his anxiety would grow worse as he contemplated how far he had to go before he reached the relative safety of his hotel room and tomorrow morning, the project's shelter.

In the terminal he would force himself to walk nonchalantly through the Panamanian immigration process. Luck stayed with him and the officers would barely glance in his direction. He would walk through the terminal, wait for his luggage, hail a cab, all without incident.   But it wasn't until he had paid the bills and handed out salaries the next day that he could draw a deep breath with any real sense of ease. He carried cash several times over the course of months, and he swears that those adventures alone took years off his life.

"Guatemala must have felt relatively safe compared to that," I say as Patrick finishes the story.

"It did," he agreed. "It was never really home, but I had people there I cared about. One in particular," he says. "Her name was Katherine. She was probably the one woman I could have married and made it work."

"So what happened?" I ask.

"The kids," he answers. "The kids happened. Life happened." But I sense it was more than that.

"Well, I've heard your version," I say. "But I think I'd like to hear hers."

CHAPTER SEVEN

Annual Christmas Letter to Friends and Benefactors

I'm listening to Christmas tapes tonight. Ever try to write a Christmas letter while looking out at a volcano and palm trees, listening to Andy Williams sing, "What Child is This?"

In my free time I've been caring for a family that lives in the barranco in the 3 de mayo neighborhood. Good kids...foolish mother. The littlest kids called me today to say that they had gone to the notorious, high-security Pavon Prison with the mother to visit her marido, and she was caught smuggling drugs into the prison. She's still in detention so I'll try to get a lawyer for her tomorrow. Dumb thing to do...trying to take drugs into Pavon...

The first time I met Patrick's former girlfriend Katherine, I was impressed by how pretty she was—petite, with strawberry blond curls and luminous, golden brown eyes. We got together by arrangement in a Bismarck bookstore on a cold December day. Katherine lives in Minneapolis now, but she was in town visiting family and agreed to talk with me as long as Patrick didn't mind.

"She's probably forgotten those days," he told me with just a hint of anxiety. I could see that the memories still mattered to him, but that he didn't want to put too much emphasis on them. He need not have worried. Even though she is married now, and the mother of two boys, those memories matter to her, too. I knew it in the first minutes of our conversation.

"I went to Guatemala as a volunteer," she began. A junior at St. Thomas University in Minnesota, Katherine planned to do what many St. Thomas juniors did—study abroad for one semester. Her major was business, but she was also studying Spanish, so she thought a stint in Central America would fulfill several purposes for her. She could explore her altruistic side by volunteering, delve into the challenging business world of non-profit operations, and really learn to communicate in Spanish. Her first plan was to join a study-abroad program in Peru, but the Shining Path guerilla movement was active in that country at the time and her parents vetoed her choice. By chance, she saw a brochure on Casa Alianza, the program that Patrick was directing in Guatemala through Covenant International Foundation. Guatemala was not exactly safe, but her parents were comforted by the fact that the program was run by somebody from home, somebody they knew and trusted. She knew of Patrick, too, although she didn't really know him personally. Their families were members of the same parish in Bismarck and Patrick had been friends with her brother. She had seen him around while growing up, but he was older than she by just enough that they hadn't traveled in the same circles. Still, she admired the work he was doing, had read his frequent letters home, and thought she could help. She applied to volunteer for a semester in Guatemala, even though Casa Alianza typically didn't take in short-term volunteers. Usually, a two-year commitment was required, but because of the family connection, Patrick agreed to let her come on board. She remained in Guatemala for about eight months that first time, working closely with the children in the orphanage.

Guatemala was a revelation to Katherine. The poverty was overwhelming, but she had expected that. What did take her by surprise was the beauty of the people.

"They were kind, battered but strong, proud, giving and humble," she says. The country surrounding the orphanage was also beautiful. She lived in a volunteer house at the base of the volcano Agua. "Every morning I would wake up and almost lose my breath taking in all the beauty." But she says the kids were just kids—loving, sweet and happy. It seemed to her as if she always had a child on each hand and another standing by waiting to offer a hug.

"You just felt like you never had enough love to share and they had mountains of love to give," she says.

When she first arrived in Guatemala she admits to being a little fearful. She had studied the history of the country and knew of its turbulent past. She knew that there was a dark side to life there. But she was quickly absorbed into the details of daily living and was too busy to really worry much about it.

"Even though Patrick founded many group homes for girls,

at the orphanage it was all boys! There were 150 of them. It was really a lot like summer camp, but everything was very well structured and well staffed," she continues. "Everyone had a job, a place to be, a person to take care of. I remember vividly spending afternoons cleaning the pig pens, herding the sheep and sweeping out the rabbit hutches with their mountains of poop, and the whole time just chatting and laughing with the kids. They even taught me how to kill chickens. They thought my ineptitude was hilarious."

The children loved to tell Patrick about her, how she chased the chickens before she could wring their necks. About how long it took her to pluck them and cook them. Patrick checked in on her frequently during those first weeks, and often invited her along when he went out, although at first they were never alone.

"He never went out to eat without having at least two kids along. Usually there were five or six, and Patrick would pick up one or two along the way, too. When a street child stepped forward outside the restaurant and offered to watch our car, Patrick would always ask the kid if he'd eaten lately. Before you knew it, that young stranger was joining us at the table."

Katherine says she was a little intimidated by Patrick and his image, a feeling that she never quite got over. "I kind of put him on a pedestal because he was clearly so important in his role there." Katherine describes a day that reinforced that first impression.

"I was on a trip with some of the kids to a remote area in Guatemala," she remembers, "and I was chatting with a local woman who asked me what I was doing in the country. When I told her I was working for Patrick, right away she lit up and said, 'Ahhh, Patricio, he is a gift from God to the people of Guatemala. He is like gold to us.' I found out later that he helped the village obtain an electrical system and street lights."

As the weeks went by, though, she says Patrick found more time to see her. He began checking in on her more often, though he continued to travel a lot and work long hours. She began to look forward to his visits and dinner invitations. And then, one weekend he asked her to accompany a group from the program to El Salvador for a business retreat. There, they finally connected.

"I was feeling more for him, but you know, sometimes you think it's one-sided and you worry about it. I think I kind of felt like he was way too important to be getting involved with me."

Insecure in close relationships himself, Patrick would tell me later that he read her caution as reluctance, and because of it, he moved slowly, trying to hold part of himself back. He knew that she was leaving at the end of her semester and he didn't want to miss her too much when she was gone. But he could not deny his growing feelings for her. He even called her from the United States when he took a rare vacation back to Bismarck.

"I was shocked!" she recalls. "Now understand, there was no phone in my house and there were no cell phones at the time.

I had to be tracked down and walk a good five-to-ten minutes to get to the phone. So when he called, I thought something was wrong, but he was just calling to check in and say hi. That got me thinking."

Katherine wasn't the only one who noticed Patrick's growing attachment. The children in the orphanage also noted it, and began to treat her as an intruder.

"They were definitely threatened," Patrick recalled. "They were afraid I would leave them for her. And we're not talking one or two or 12 kids here, we're talking hundreds. They were afraid she and I would spend all of our time together and not include them, so they began to treat her poorly."

Finally, Patrick gathered them all together and explained the situation. "I started out by telling them that I loved them and would always love them. But I also told them that I cared very much about Katherine, in a different way, a way that wasn't going to affect the way I loved them. I ended by asking their permission to be a special friend with her and they agreed. They never gave her any trouble after that." Patrick also told the children that Katherine was going to leave when the school year was over.

"She will leave," he said, "but I will stay here with you."

And Patrick was right. Katherine finished up her year and returned to St. Thomas to spend her senior year in Minnesota and to graduate. Before she left, though, her presence had an unexpected effect.

"I don't know if it was her, if it was the fact that I was finally opening up and sharing with someone," he told me, "or if it would have happened anyway, but some of the stresses and terrible memories of the years before started to come back on me in a big way. The first time it happened, we had been enjoying the evening together."

ANTIGUA, GUATEMALA
1987

Darkness fell quickly on Antigua. Surrounded as it is by volcanoes, it can be sunny one minute, shadowy the next, and profoundly dark just moments after that, with only moonlight to see by. Patrick and Katherine were walking in the twilight of a summer evening. He looked exhausted. She could see dark circles under his eyes. He'd been sick a lot lately, with stomach bugs and fevers that he had picked up on his travels, and she knew he never got enough sleep. She worried about him.

"Why do you do this, Patrick?" she finally asked, though she was nervous that he would see her concern as prying. Still, she persisted. "Why do you put yourself at risk? Most people consider it a job and walk away at the end of the day, but not you."

She wasn't the first to ask, of course, and usually he ignored the question and changed the subject, but her timing was right. He had been asking himself the same questions lately, and he needed to tell someone, to trust someone with his feelings.

"I think it's the faces," he finally said. "They haunt my dreams. I think about how these people are suffering, and I realize that God is putting me in a position where I can take away some of that pain. I know I can't help everyone, but I dream about those—people I know I can help. It's as if God hired me to be the emergency room doctor for these bloody, violent countries we're working in."

They neared the stone-lined well that sat behind Katherine's house. Patrick peered into the well, then turned around and leaned his hips against the small housing that held the well bucket. Reaching across, he pulled Katherine into the circle of his arms, and she leaned back into him. The words didn't come easily at first, but finally, he spoke.

"I keep seeing the faces of all of those kids I tried to help when I first arrived, when the war was at its worst," he whispered. "It's as if every time we turned a corner, there would be another smoking village or another dead body lying by the side of the road. And usually, there were kids there, just standing around wailing, or worse yet, expressionless and not making a sound. Their faces were always full of terror and confusion. More than anything, I wanted to take that look off their faces. I still do. I want to give them back their childhoods, give them back their dreams, if that's possible."

It was the same feeling that had drawn him to work in New York–that desire to help. But here, small changes made such big differences. Here, an elementary education could mean the difference between a lifetime of poverty and despair and a real future with a job that paid a living wage. Nothing could make these kids forget the horror of the war, but many of the children he rescued did well in school and were heading for graduation and a better life. He felt good about the difference he was making.

But Katherine also saw the toll his work was taking. He frequently wore a haunted expression, and he closely guarded his emotions. He had already said more about himself tonight than he had in the entire time she'd known him, and because she thought it might help, she encouraged him to keep talking. "You know, you never tell me about those experiences, and you don't talk much about the places you've been," she continued. "You must have seen some terrible things."

Patrick stared first at Katherine, and then out into the darkness. He couldn't remember ever having stopped to really think about all that he had gone through. Like a fireman or an ambulance driver, he had just reacted to the scenes that he had come across—the children dying and laid at his feet; the screaming mob in Haiti; the explosion in El Salvador; the bone-chilling fear that he felt every time he was stopped at a military checkpoint on an isolated country road.

Finally, for the first time ever, he began to talk about some of the things he had witnessed. He told her about the villages that he had seen burned to the ground—about the crying mothers and the newly dug graves. About the medicines and clothing he had smuggled in to people who were sick and dying in El Salvador, and of the blankets he had sent into the Guatemalan mountains because innocent Mayan Indian people hiding there were wet and almost always cold. And about the time he had driven into a ditch to avoid hitting three headless corpses left lying in the road in El Salvador, only to remember that ditches like these were often land-mined.

Like hers, his commitment to be a lay missionary in Guatemala had only been for six months, he told her, but after only three, he hadn't known how he could leave. There was so much work to do.

He talked about one harrowing scene after another and seemed lost in the memories. She was sure he had forgotten she was even there. He seemed so far away, and it frightened her. The night grew cold and she shivered.

"Hey!" she finally said, and he blinked a few times, returning to the moment. He stood up abruptly.

"I'd better get you home," he said. "It's late."

Spent, Patrick walked her back to her house before returning to his office at the orphanage. He felt drained. He put his feet up on the desk, put a cassette in the stereo; and, as he listened to Manfred Mann play *Blinded by the Light*, he acknowledged that he was tired. It was spring in North Dakota. The ice would just be melting on the Missouri River. He wanted to go home.

Life was not the same for Patrick after that evening spent talking to Katherine by the star-lit well. The "wall" that had separated him, that he had built to protect himself from all he was living through, had developed a crack that was now growing wider. Nightmares of the violence and bloodshed soon started to haunt him every night. Panic attacks gripped him during the day when he drove the same roads that he had driven during the war. Sometimes the panic hit without warning—sparked by a familiar face, a sad expression. He never knew what would bring back the memories that he had buried. When it happened, he would feel his breathing grow labored, almost as if someone were tightening a belt around his chest. His heart would race. Normal, everyday sounds, if they were loud enough, would make him jump and feel like hiding. Idling cars along the streets reminded him of the horrors of the disappearances he had seen and heard about, and of people he had worked with who had been tortured and killed or later released. He would find himself scanning his surroundings, looking for hidden dangers, searching for a secondary way out. Little by little, he began to admit to himself that the war years had taken their toll.

Katherine had to face her own reality that night. She loved Patrick. She had only recently realized just how much. And, she was fairly certain that he loved her too, even if he didn't or couldn't recognize it. But perhaps love wasn't enough. She wasn't sure that the two of them could ever make a life together. She was starting to understand what he had been trying to tell her for months. His life was his work—his commitment was to Christ and his family was the poor. She could see that he would never be able to turn his back on them. Not for her, not for anybody. The question was, could she share him with that world? Besides, he had not spoken to her of love. Perhaps, she thought, he needed time to sort out his feelings and decide what he wanted from life. Perhaps that's what she needed to do, too.

When she finished her semester and boarded the plane home, he kissed her goodbye and walked away. He did not look back. He knew that if he were to survive on his own, he had to begin the process of rebuilding his wall, of containing his feelings. What Katherine couldn't know then, was that though they would see each other again, and though she would work with him after graduation and continue on as a lay missionary herself, things would never be the same. Perhaps without even realizing it, Patrick had let her go.

What he couldn't walk away from, though, was the change that had started in him that night by the well. He had opened a Pandora's Box of memories that were somehow sapping his energy. He was losing his drive and he knew it. He admitted to himself that it was time to leave, to go home, and he wrote his letter of resignation. First, he wanted to make sure that the children he had taken in were going to be taken care of, and then he planned to take up his life in North Dakota again.

But instead, CIF offered him a job traveling through Southeast Asia, assessing different countries for expansion of the programs that he had founded in Central America. After a great deal of thought and prayer, he decided that this was a way he could help.

"The program in Guatemala was fiscally sound and doing well. It was basically running itself and there were few challenges," he says as we flip through photo albums from those early days. He points out picture after picture of beautiful children with Asian faces, the street children of Thailand, Vietnam and Malaysia. "What I needed was something that would completely occupy my thoughts and exhaust me to the point where I didn't dream. I was running from the demons of war," he adds. "I thought these children might be the answer."

He accepted the job, said goodbye to all of the children he had grown to love in Guatemala, and with a promise to remain a part of their lives, he moved to Singapore. What would follow were two years of non-stop travel and constant work that in the end, would yield little fruit and cause Patrick a lot of grief.

At the same time, Katherine graduated from St. Thomas, and moved to Japan to study. Once again they were in the same corner of the world, but they rarely saw one another. Patrick wrote her letters that he never sent.

Dear Katherine,

I can't believe how much I miss you! The time that you've been gone seems like a lifetime. I have some news to pass along. As you know, I resigned my position as executive director here at the project, effective in May or once a replacement can be found.

I'm not sure what life will bring next, but since my resignation, I've been asked to consider opening several new programs in the Far East over the next four or five years. I think I'll take the job, and if I do, I'll spend six weeks in each of the following eight places doing needs assessments, program networking, cost-of-living and program indexes and photography: Philippines, Singapore, Australia, Vietnam, Thailand, Bangladesh, India and Pakistan. I'll spend the first several months traveling alone trying to research and photograph the underground worlds of child slavery, child prostitution and street life as it exists in these countries.

Not much more that I can say about the job, as it's still undefined, but I'm shell-shocked just thinking about it. It's undefined because we've never done anything like this before, so we really don't know what to look forward to. And I feel shell-shocked because at the same time, I was really looking forward to getting back to the States and starting a normal life. I'm turning 30 in another 60 days, and I can really feel the wear and tear I've put on this poor body in both my heart and bones. Like I mentioned in my last letter, I'm now beginning to fear loneliness more than I would ever have guessed.

I wonder if I really can start all over again. Not that studying the languages, cultures, people or kids would be impossible— but simply put, I don't know if I have the strength to pack up, get on a plane by myself and step off alone for x number of years in a place as foreign to me as the Far East. Que Dios entienda y me disculpe por mis debilidades.

Anyway, since you left, I've spent most evenings walking the neighborhoods alone, wondering what you're doing. One good thing about this Asia assignment—at least I'll be in your part of the world. Perhaps we can get together in Singapore, or we can meet up somewhere else for a visit. Write me Kath. I miss you.

Love, Patrick

CHAPTER EIGHT

Letter to Most Rev. John F. Kinney, Bishop of Bismarck

Your Excellency;

Thanks for your letter. You asked how my trip to Vietnam was. Vietnam is a beautiful country, both physically and otherwise. That beauty, though, masks an unbelievable poverty. Per capita income is less than $100 a year, and you see the decaying infrastructure everywhere. People beg from the few tourists who are there. Even little babies automatically stretch out an open hand when they see a tourist.

It's hard to believe this war ended for us over 16 years ago.

As I may have explained in my last letter, in each country my job is to make the initial contacts with church, government, embassy and professional entities. I also try to record and photograph the street activities of homeless children, and the plight of poor women caught up in what is known as white slavery. These visits and accompanying photos, maps, economic studies, etc., eventually form a site report which details the basis for a hypothetical program for that particular city, or the reasons why we would not want to become involved. Since this is this charity's first overture in the region, each of these contacts could properly be termed a "cold call." The reaction from most is generally receptive, although I sometimes feel as though I might as well be carrying a Fuller brush in my hand.

I spent most of my time in Vietnam visiting officials, seeing the other hospitals and orphanages, listening and looking. I took one day to go into the Mekong Delta region where I photographed orphaned kids working in the rice fields. Since that area is so wet and flat and swampy, it was largely left out of the war, although it, too, saw its share of violence. You can still feel the innocence of the soil and can tell that the people are "more whole" than the people in Ho Chi Minh City and points north.

A day later I rented a car and went into the Cu Chi free-fire zone that lies about 90 kilometers north of Saigon. This area was overrun and deeply tunneled by the Viet Cong, who then used it as an operational, supply, and hospital base. For many of the people who had lived there before the war began, their lives and land will never be the same. Many are blind or missing a limb—bomb craters still pock the earth, downed helicopters and disabled tanks still litter the fields, and scorched tree stumps jut out from the more recent growth. Few crops will grow because of the thousands of tons of chemicals that were dumped. Even the water that is desperately needed to bring about a rebirth of the soil is contaminated.

One afternoon I went walking through a rice field where I saw the shell of a personnel carrier. Walking towards it, I noticed that there were about a dozen small children playing inside. They laughed and ran and were having a great time. They couldn't have cared less about the war. They probably didn't even know that it had ever existed. The kids' laughter reminded me that time, as both a healer and an anesthetic, was once again performing a small miracle.

This is quite a job that I have here, and certainly different from trying to raise several hundred kids in Central America. In Central America I knew that I was sowing the seeds for a future harvest. In Asia, however, I realize that I am barely scratching at the topsoil (while using a very small stick!).

During these trips, I find that my compassion for the poor intensifies with almost every step. There is so much that can be done with so very little. The need is so overwhelming that I must constantly remind myself that "the poor will always be with us" or else I risk losing perspective and face burn-out. Your support and prayers help so much and mean everything to me.

Sincerely,
Patrick Atkinson, 1989

Patrick stands Carlitos up in the hallway to take his picture with a digital camera. He has received an e-mail from Dr. Mickelson in Bismarck, asking for the child's medical details. Kevin has promised to take the case to the hospital administration, but first he wants to know what they'll be working with. Patrick gathers as much information as he can from Carlitos' cousin and from Dr. Luis Enrique, the Guatemalan pediatrician who staffs the Dreamer Center Clinic on a part-time, volunteer basis. He had examined Carlitos when he was first brought in. Patrick believes a photograph of the boy will help explain the story, and will also make him seem more real to the hospital administration. And it's true, it would be difficult to say no to a child with a face like this one.

First, Patrick takes a full-length shot of Carlitos. Next he takes close-ups of the healing bullet wounds in his tiny body and of the site where the catheter pokes through the little boy's abdomen. Finally, he takes a close-up shot of Carlitos' smiling face. Carlitos smiles in every picture. Even when tears fill his eyes, he attempts to please and befriend. No doubt about it, this is a charming kid.

Months later, over a cup of cappuccino in a Bismarck café, Dr. Mickelson would tell me that he could remember the exact moment he decided to try to help Carlitos. He was tired that day, he remembered, just leaving from a 14-hour shift in the Emergency Department at Bismarck's St. Alexius Medical Center. He said he saw the message light blinking on his phone and thought he'd ignore it. But something, he doesn't know what, compelled him to drop his jacket in a chair and punch in the code for his messages. And there was the voice-mail from Patrick Atkinson, telling him about the boy and asking him to check his e-mail. "I turned to the computer, opened the attachment from Guatemala, and there he was…this full-screen picture of that beautiful little boy with the bloody catheter protruding from his belly," he said.

"I just remember thinking, 'Oh my God, there's no way to not help this kid," Kevin added. Without a moment's hesitation, he said he typed out the response, "Patrick, I'll see what I can do," and hit the command to "Send."

The next day Dr. Mickelson sent Patrick's e-mail to the administrators at St. Alexius Medical Center, explaining the situation and asking for permission to take the case pro bono. He received it, and before the day was out, Dr. Mickelson had talked with specialists who were busy gathering a team of physicians, nurses and administrators willing to try their best to help. Word about this small boy's painful ordeal and Patrick's public plea for help filled the hospital's hallways and people called Dr. Mickelson, volunteering to house Carlitos, offering donations of clothing, toys and money—even offering to adopt him. "But first," Dr. Mickelson told me, "I knew we had to get him to the United States." Everywhere he went, Kevin showed people the photographs of Carlitos' smiling face.

This is not the first time Patrick has used photographs to report on a child's progress or welfare. It once seemed as if he'd taken a picture of every street child in Southeast Asia, trying to get the world's benefactors to care enough to donate the cash to feed and house them. Even as he struggled to keep from becoming cynical, Patrick had learned an important lesson during those difficult years—that people respond more readily when the request comes from somebody they know and with a picture attached.

"Most people want to help," he tells me again and again. "They just don't know how. My job is to give them a way."

SAIGON, VIETNAM
1989

The water that poured from the tap into the hotel room bathtub was brown with pollution and smelled of sewage, but tonight at least it was hot. Patrick lowered himself into the bath. Trying to ignore the stabbing pain in his neck, he allowed his mind to drift into old memories. He thought of a time when he had been about 7 years old, and was playing with friends in Bismarck, in the old root cellar of a nearby house. As he climbed out of the cellar, one of the other children let the heavy oak planking that made up the trap door slam down on his head, knocking him unconscious. The other children, terrified that he was dead and afraid that they would be in trouble, had run off, leaving him lying alone at the base of the steps. He awoke a half hour later, barely able to move. Later, the doctor would tell his mother that he had cracked vertebrae in his neck.

That impairment, coupled with a teenage back injury that also left him with cracked vertebrae—this time between his shoulder blades—had continued to pain him into adulthood. At first, Patrick had assumed that today's back pain was a flare-up of those old injuries. But his body aches and generally sick feeling were growing worse by the minute. In the last hour, he had also developed a fever headache. One minute he was shivering so hard that his jaw locked up, and he felt certain that his teeth were chipping. The next, he was burning up, with sweat pouring down his face. At the moment, he was in the chill phase. The hot water seemed to help. He had been vomiting, too, and he had tried to convince himself that it was part of his recurrent battle with the stomach bugs he always seemed to harbor. But instinct from years of working on the streets told him it was something worse.

During his travels across Southeast Asia and now in Vietnam, Patrick had been as careful as he knew how to be. He stayed in the best hotels he could afford, ate only in hotel restaurants, and wore long pants and long sleeves whenever he went out into the night air, despite the sweltering heat, to avoid mosquitoes. But all he had to do was turn on the tap to be reminded of how perilous this journey could be. He couldn't see the bacterial zoo swirling in the brown water that surrounded him, but he could smell it. He had been told to expect illness if he spent any length of time in Vietnam. He had been advised to never let the water near his mouth. He brushed his teeth with bottled water, and if that wasn't available, he used bottled Coca Cola, but apparently it hadn't been enough. Alone and scared, he lay in the pungent bath for most of the night, hoping for relief. By morning, he knew he was sick with malaria.

Suddenly lightheaded and knowing that he was drifting in and out of a feverish sleep he decided it would be wiser to climb out of the bath. Most of the people he knew who contracted malaria didn't actually die from it, but he thought that if he stayed where he was for very much longer there was a very real chance that he might pass out and drown. He stepped out, clinging to the side of the tub for a long minute, waiting for the room to stop spinning. He vomited again, choked down several aspirin and slunk toward his bed. This was one illness he had particularly hoped to avoid, because it meant that the organism would remain in his bloodstream for life. The malaria would be a constant reminder of his idealistic youth, he thought with a wry smile, or of some wonderful years serving in the front lines of God's army. Oh well, he thought, at least malaria had a more romantic ring to it than amoebas, dysentery or head lice, all of which he had contracted many times.

He wasn't sure which of his many illnesses had been the worst so far. Dengue fever, perhaps. He had caught that while setting up a program for street children in Mexico City. Dengue, he later found out, is also known as "The Bone Breaker Fever" because the high and chaotic fever spikes often cause the muscle groups to spasm in different directions, snapping the bones to which they are attached. Once again, he had been working alone in the dangerous slums of Mexico City.

That time, Patrick had wrapped himself in several layers of blankets and alternated between calling for beverages from room service and asking for a doctor. Finally, after three days, the hotel doctor arrived.

"It's definitely dengue fever," the doctor said, "and it's not something you can ignore. It may actually kill you unless you receive immediate and proper care," he added. His first concern, however, was not for the young patient lying before him soaked in his own sweat, but for the hotel's responsibility if Patrick should die there.

"Do you know anyone in Mexico?" the doctor asked Patrick. "If you don't, then we should get you home quickly or else you will go to a hospital and you could stay there among strangers for a very long time."

A barely-coherent Patrick could not remember the name of a single person whom he knew or with whom he had worked in Mexico City, so the doctor searched Patrick's belongings and papers until he found his passport and airline ticket.

"I see here that you are scheduled on a flight that leaves tomorrow at 2:00 in the afternoon. I think you should be on it."

Patrick did not see how that was possible, but the doctor seemed confident. "The airport is an hour from here. I'll be back at 10:00 in the morning to help you," he told Patrick before leaving for the night.

As promised, the hotel doctor returned to Patrick's room the next day, along with the hotel's general manager. The manager showed Patrick a bill for his stay, which included a $200 charge for the doctor's two visits, and asked him how he intended to pay. Still delirious and dehydrated, Patrick said nothing. The hotel doctor once again reached into the travel pack where Patrick kept his ticket and travel papers, and where he also kept his wallet and credit card.

"Ah, this should work," the hotel manager said, removing one of the credit cards and leaving the room.

With the hotel manager gone, the doctor reached into his coat pocket and pulled out a long syringe.

"After I give you this injection, Patrick, you are going to feel strange. You are going to feel as if you are floating. I can send you to a hospital here, and that's what I should do, but you've said you don't know anyone here. So, I'm going to give you this shot, and then the hotel staff is going to help you pack your bags and drive you to the airport. When you get to the counter, just give them your ticket, show them your passport, and get on the plane. Go home. Go immediately to a hospital when you get there," the doctor said. "Do you understand?"

Patrick nodded, then asked the doctor to write down the name of the medicine he had just been injected with.

"Can't do that," the doctor said. When Patrick asked for a receipt or at least for his name, the doctor smiled and said, "Can't do that either. I'm giving you this shot so that you can make it onto the plane. Trust me. You'll be all right, so long as you follow my instructions. Now, good-bye, and travel well."

Patrick had made it home that time, but he remembered very little about the drive to the airport, the flight back, or how he got from the airport to the hospital.

This time, as he lay alone in his hotel room in downtown

Ho Chi Minh City, he again thought to himself that dengue fever had definitely been worse. But this was pretty bad.

He spent days recovering and eventually, the fever subsided enough so that he was able to fly home to Singapore, but the malaria hit him again a short time later, and once again Patrick found himself curled up on the floor mattress where he slept, sick and alone. He pulled a sheet over his legs, still shivering despite the sticky, wet heat. As he lay there in the semi-darkness, his thoughts were far from this South China Sea island-state. A Jefferson Starship classic played on the radio, and he missed his friends and family back home in Bismarck.

He was also filled with a new anxiety. He had been receiving letters from the children he had raised for seven years in Central America, telling him that there had been changes in the programs that he had founded. They said they were not getting along with the staff or the new director, and that they were afraid they would be kicked out of the orphanage. When Patrick tried to find out what was going on there, he received no answers. In fact, he had noticed an ominous silence from the home office—too many questions had gone unanswered. Something didn't feel right. But he couldn't muster the strength to do anything about it. He could hear his own labored breathing.

"What happens if I die here?" he wondered to himself. "Would anyone notice?" He asked the question of God, but didn't discern an answer. Trying not to think about the fever and the doubts that wracked his brain, he eventually and mercifully drifted off to sleep.

He was awakened later by a persistent knocking at the door that at first he thought was part of his headache. When it didn't go away he forced his eyes open and looked around. It was light outside. He had no idea how long he had been asleep, or who could be trying to get in. He knew almost nobody in Singapore, since this was only the base from which he worked across Southeast Asia. He dragged himself to the door, his head swirling, pulled it open and stood for a long moment trying to focus on the person standing there. It was the strawberry blonde hair that finally tipped him off. It was Katherine.

"You're here!" he said.

"Of course I'm here, you invited me," she said impatiently, but then stopped and reached out a hand to touch his forehead. "You look awful. How long have you been sick?"

"I don't know. What day is it?"

"Tuesday. Patrick, please tell me you've seen a doctor." she said, stepping into the room.

"Meaning to," he replied before walking the few steps back to his bed and lying down again. The light hurt his eyes. "As soon as I feel better."

"What is it? Parasites? Malaria?" she asked. Now working in Japan, she too had been a missionary long enough to know that malaria was an ever-present threat in these hot, humid climates.

"That's my guess." He smiled at her. "It's great to see you, though. Come on in," he said faintly, before drifting off to sleep again.

For the next several days, Katherine stayed with him until he was better. She got him to eat a little and they had the chance to visit. She told him what she'd been doing in Japan, and he shared his impressions of all the things he'd seen—beautiful countries devastated by wars and poverty and the poverty-driven trading of children and women.

"The saddest sights I've seen were probably at the Subic Bay whorehouses," he told her. "Beautiful girls and boys who know no other way of life. We're talking tiny kids here. Second, third, fourth generation prostitutes. They are born into it."

He also told her about the confusing letters he had been receiving from the corporate headquarters, followed by long silences. For a long time he had felt a growing sense that all was not well within the organization, and his fears were now apparently coming to pass. Katherine didn't know much more than Patrick did about what was happening back in the charity's corporate offices, but she too had heard that there were serious allegations being made and growing talk of a scandal among the charity's leadership back in New York City.

"But so far nothing official," she said, "so maybe nothing will happen." They tried to talk of other things, but both were worried about what the future held.

When Katherine left to return to Japan she was more

confused than ever about her relationship with Patrick. He had been sick, of course, but even as he began to feel better he was distant and distracted. When he looked at her now, she got the distinct feeling that he wasn't really seeing her at all.

CHAPTER NINE

Letter home, Spring 1990

Dear Mom and Dad,

By now you've probably heard about the scandal with the agency that I've been working with. It's been in all the papers. I heard about it in Singapore by watching CNN, and it explained a lot. Anyway, the long and the short of it is, I'm finished working with them, and I'm coming home...

Patrick is a saver. He has kept copies of nearly every letter he's ever written or received, from childhood on. He stores them all jumbled together in boxes in a musty basement. For several weeks last winter I sorted through them—birthday cards, old letters from high school girlfriends, words of advice from his grandmother, and letters home. Those letters, more than anything else, convince me that Patrick's mission is almost as old as he is. His goals have never changed. He puts one foot in front of the other, doing what he believes God asks him to do, and he will continue to do so until the work is done or until God tells him to stop.

He has also saved all of the e-mails he's received, every

photograph he's taken, every heartfelt gift he's been given, even his childhood books. He owns an entire shelf full of biographies about St. John Bosco, books he purchased as a child, with money he earned through after-school and summer jobs.

In a fire-resistant metal cabinet, he also has a file at least three inches thick on a scandal that happened a half a world away, in New York City, at the offices of Covenant House International. The scandal had nothing to do with him, and yet the fallout forced him to change course in his career, and very nearly caused him to give up mission work altogether.

"They trashed me," Patrick says. I am flipping through the file and he is at his Dreamer Center desk, trying to sign checks to pay project bills, but now that I've asked him a question about Covenant House, he sets down his pen and leans forward, giving me his full attention. "I was in Southeast Asia when the scandal hit and they offered me a desk job back in New York. I suppose they wanted to see which side of the fence I'd be on, and when I came down on the side of the truth, they set out to destroy me—to destroy my credibility, my reputation and my life."

He has never been able to completely forget it—the unfairness of it. The way he sees it, he had given years of his life to building a better future for poor people, risking his own skin again and again, only to have it nearly end with rumors and whispering.

"One day I was lunching with cardinals and presidents. The next, I was defending my work and fighting off rumors that

I had somehow misused my position to profit from the poor. At the time I just kept thinking it was all a horrible misunderstanding, and that if only I could talk to somebody I could clear it all up, but all of the doors that were formerly wide open were suddenly closed."

It's a subject he still doesn't like to talk about. Even now, it causes him sleepless nights. He believes that it comes down to the basic battle between good and evil. He is winning it, but he's never entirely free of its effects.

"For a while, my faith in people was shaken," Patrick says "but I never lost the belief that God would pull me through it. Still, it was hell." And he was angry – angry enough to return home and get a job shoveling asphalt. He turned his back on his old life, but then, one day he was forced to take his own words to heart. When the good run from the bad, the bad win.

BISMARCK, NORTH DAKOTA
Summer 1990

The sweat dripped off Patrick's face and stung his eyes, but he didn't bother to wipe it away. There was little point. Sweat was simply part of his day at the hot and steamy North Dakota State Highway Department asphalt plant and nothing was going to stop it. As he climbed the thousand-degree tar burners and worked with the scalding, sticky tar, he could feel the strain across the muscles of his back, but he welcomed that too. The harder he worked, the less time he had to think. He was usually surprised when the whistle blew and it was time to start shutting the plant down, because he had spent the day far away, off in some dream world where his mind was asleep, his actions on autopilot.

He put in for all of the overtime that the State of North Dakota would give him, but he couldn't work 24 hours a day. It was only after he laid down his shovel, grabbed his lunch pail and joined the line of workers clocking out that he realized just how exhausted he really was. As he climbed into the Highway Department truck and headed for home, he would wrinkle his nose at his own smell, and pick at the sticky tar that hung from different parts of his well-worn clothing.

Since beginning his new job, he sometimes wondered if the odor of hot tar was permanently burned onto him. His task was to sample and test the asphalt that would become the new highway surface. It didn't take a lot of skill, yet he enjoyed it. He liked the fact that he could leave it behind at the end of the day. It was a stress-free job and he needed that. He was also thrilled to have new friends with whom he could talk, drink "cold ones," and shoot pool after work. None of the friends knew about the international work he had been doing just months before, and he was delighted to keep it that way.

"What's behind me is behind me," Patrick thought. "From here forward, it's a whole new life." But it was a life for which he was ill equipped.

Returning home from Singapore had been more difficult than Patrick had anticipated. He had been on his own since high school, first going to Minnesota State University-Moorhead, then moving right into a worldwide service ministry shortly after graduation. He had never had to learn many of the day-to-day survival and social skills that most young adults take for granted. He didn't know how to choose and buy a car for himself, or how to rent an American apartment. The few pieces of furniture that he had brought home from his travels overseas he had found to be infested with termites, so he threw them out. He was stunned to see what replacement pieces would cost him.

"I can't spend that much money," he once shouted at a startled sales clerk. "Do you realize I can build an entire house in Central America for the price of that sofa set?" he asked another before storming out of a store.

He felt he couldn't go back, but he also found it difficult to go forward. The first sign that Patrick's transition into a more ordinary life was not going to be easy came just three days after he moved into a new apartment, and less than 12 hours after his phone service had been connected. He received a telephone call from the American Drug Enforcement Agency, asking him how his work in Southeast Asia had gone and welcoming him back to the United States.

They told him they were looking for people who understood Central American and Southeast Asian politics, they knew of his international work and they offered to fly him to

Washington for a job interview. Surprising as it was, the call made sense. Patrick had a degree in criminal justice and intimate knowledge of the way the system worked in the Third World— yet it bothered him that someone from an agency with which he'd had no contact would know enough about him to know the number on a phone that had been so recently installed. It gave him the eerie feeling of being watched, and he wanted nothing to do with it.

At the same time, acquaintances and friends from the charity where he had worked for so many years began to call and write frequently, and what he heard was not good. They told him that rumors were being floated about him, to the effect that there had been mismanagement in his programs overseas, programs that he knew to be sound—and other talk, so farfetched that it would have seemed ridiculous had there not been such an evil, sinister feel to it. He recalled the lessons from individuals at Covenant House about how to survive a crisis situation. Their motto was to deny, discredit, and destroy any accusers. What he couldn't believe was that they appeared to now be doing this to him.

At first he thought there must be some horrible misunderstanding, but when he tried to contact the right people to straighten things out, he met a solid wall of resistance. His calls were never returned, his former employers were never in, his letters asking for clarifications and resolutions went mostly answered. Patrick believed the warnings that he was being portrayed in a bad light, but since he was on his own in his Midwestern hometown, he couldn't seem to find the right means to defend himself. The horror of what was happening kept him awake at night as he tried to come to grips with the overwhelming sense of injustice he felt at the things that apparently were being said about him. One East Coast reporter tracked him down to ask if it was true that he had worked for the Central Intelligence Agency. Another wanted to know if he had supported the Guatemalan leftist guerillas.

Almost without realizing it, he slowly began to lose the desire and the energy to leave his apartment. Trips out to buy food or to see his family and friends became less and less frequent, and when people knocked on his door, he usually didn't answer. Each day seemed to bring worse news.

On top of that was a sense of helplessness at what was happening to those he had left behind. Letters came almost daily from the children he had cared for in Central America, saying that many of them were now living, and dying, on the streets and in the alleys of Guatemala. They told him the new head of Casa Alianza was spreading horrible rumors about him, while all the time continuing to write Patrick friend-to-friend letters.

Wondering out loud where God had gone in all of this, Patrick began to spend entire days lying alone on the floor of his nearly empty apartment, staring at the ceiling, watching helplessly as the life that he had spent a decade building crumbled around him. To one old friend he wrote:

Dear Jean,

I don't recall when I last wrote to you, but my life has turned completely upside down since then. As you have probably heard or read in the news, the agency is in deep trouble and the scandal in their corporate offices seems to be running pretty rampant.

So how does this affect me? They decided to cut the newer direct-care programs. Asia, being the farthest away and also the newest, was axed. They told me on February 2, and it became effective on February 28. They said I had to find my own way home from Southeast Asia since they were busy with other things. They offered me a new position back in New York, but I was so appalled by what I saw there that I said 'no.' Since then, they've not only cut me loose, they're doing their best to discredit me.

So...where does this leave me after working in the ditches for them for over a decade? Lost actually. I don't know what I'm going to do. This was never a job; it was a vocation, an expression of belief. What I did, I did for Christ and for the poor. There's tremendous merit in that. It would be impossible to overstate the feeling that I've been deceived...

It took awhile, but finally, Patrick's friends began to notice that something was seriously wrong. They knew he was back in Bismarck, and yet they never heard from him. An old high school friend, Scott McFall, tried for days to call him, but when his calls went unanswered he finally decided to drop by unannounced. He saw Patrick's car in the driveway and assumed he was home, but nobody came to the door when he knocked. He tried twice more, then shrugged and walked around to the back of the apartment building where he could see through the sliding glass doors. He spotted Patrick asleep on the floor.

"Hey Pat! I can see you in there. What's up? Are you asleep?" No response. "Pat? OK, I'm coming in!" He turned the handle and found the door unlocked. Patrick glanced up at him, but didn't get up or acknowledge him. He simply turned away. Scott glanced around. The apartment was in disarray. Patrick himself was unshaven and disheveled. There were dark circles under his eyes. The mail was spread out on the floor around him, letters that either vilified him or begged him for help. Either way, he felt powerless.

Scott insisted he get up and get dressed, and nagged him until he agreed to go out. As the two of them sat at a table in a local bar, Patrick poured out his problems and Scott listened intently, never interrupting. Finally, when Patrick finished, he was quiet for a moment before offering surprisingly simple, yet effective advice. He told Patrick to quit moping around, to stop waiting for the mail and find a job. Even if it was something mindless, his friend told him, it would get him out of his apartment and focused on something else.

"So they tried to discredit you," he said. "You'll live through that. They're the ones under investigation, not you. Those who truly know you won't believe it. I don't believe it." Then he gave Patrick back a little of his own advice. He told him, "God doesn't demand that you succeed, he simply asks you to try. You're the one who told me that. You tried and you did a hell of a job. Now pull yourself together."

It was the right advice at the right time. The next day Patrick answered a want ad for an asphalt plant job, zeroing in on work that was purely physical. He spent his days making sure that the asphalt would hold up under North Dakota's harsh climate. There was something immensely satisfying about that. He worked long hours, and often woke at two or three in the morning in order to get out to a distant job site long before sunrise, when his day's work began. He would rise when the world was cloaked in darkness, his muscles still stiff and sore from the previous day's work. He'd climb into his used Audi, crank up his stereo to chase the sleep from his brain and drive to meet the rest of his crew. Then they all drove to the site together.

Their early morning chat was minimal—usually just a comment about a party that somebody had attended or sleepy laughter over a woman that someone had met. Sometimes the ride was entirely silent—the only sound coming from the car's engine and the radio.

The weather was sticky hot that summer, but nothing that Patrick couldn't handle after his months in Southeast Asia. The North Dakota mornings were wonderfully cool and calm. It was the favorite part of Patrick's day, so long as he kept his thoughts away from New York and Guatemala.

As the weeks passed, Patrick began to look for ways to fill

up his off hours, too. He applied to law schools, and while he waited to hear from them, began practicing martial arts with friends.

He bought a HUD duplex, and decided that learning to fix it up would be therapeutic. He telephoned Julette Brodehl, a local girl he had dated once before, and soon the two of them were going out for pizza, movies, and late-night dancing. Slowly, the fog that had surrounded him began to lift.

Even though the letters from New York and Guatemala continued to come in, and he continued to hear about rumors designed to discredit him and keep him isolated from the Covenant House investigation, his attitude had changed. No longer willing to be a victim, when he was contacted by federal investigators looking for information about the charity, he told them what he knew. It was cathartic. He was finally able to sleep again. His health returned and he knew that his prayers had been heard. God had been with him all along.

CHAPTER TEN

Letter from Guatemala

July 3, 1990

Dear Patrick,

For me it's a pleasure to take my paper and pen and greet you, wishing you good health at the side of your appreciative family.

I want to thank you for the money and birthday present that you sent me—and for the card. The stickers are very nice. Everyone likes the present of the dragon, and I especially like it.

I want to tell you that everything is going well in school. I have had some problems, but nothing unusual. Last month I failed two classes but I'm going to make them up. I wanted to ask if you would still help me by paying for school since the money you left has run out. Also, I was sick but thanks be to God I'm better. Alejandro is not with us any longer.

Everything has changed in my life. It's not the same as when you were here. Everybody loved you although sometimes we stole from you, but we still loved you as a father.

I want to ask you to send me photos of when you are working, water skiing and boating on the river. Although we are far apart I love you like a father, like the father that I never had.

Well, Papito, this is what has happened during these past months. I'm sorry for not having written earlier. Every night

I pray to our Creator for you, that you are taken care of during
good times and bad, and that nothing happens to you. I love
you very much, Papito.

See you soon,
Walter Luna

———————————

Learning to work the system doesn't come overnight,
especially in a country like Guatemala, where corruption seems
cyclical, depending on who is in power at the time. It begins at
the local level. Nepotism is a way of life, as is bribery, paternalism
and discrimination. Patrick has made many friends along the
way by being generous with his time and talent and through his
unflagging devotion to the poor and destitute of Guatemala, so
when he needs to call in a favor, there are places he can turn for
help. It's at times like these, he tells me, that those favors can
prove vital. Patrick is scheduled to speak to a group of volunteers
just coming in from Holland, but he is waylaid by Sonia
Xinico…who tells him that there is a serious hitch in Carlitos'
paperwork.

"The prosecutor in the case has asked the judge not to allow
him to leave until he has testified. That could take months," she
says. She tells him she spent the day at the (minister of justice)
office, trying to gain permission for a temporary visa.

"He says that without Carlitos, they may not have a case,"
she adds.

Patrick grabs the keys to the Dreamer Center's big white van and we head for the door. He has decided that he will try to talk with the Assistant Attorney General himself. It is a private visit, so I wait on a long, wooden bench on the veranda outside the judge's office, admiring the view of volcanoes in the distance and watching the slow pace of business on a Guatemalan afternoon. I am asked three times, by boys of various ages, if I would like my shoes shined. I am wearing white Adidas sneakers.

Two hours later, Patrick has a tentative agreement. He tells me that the judge has agreed to allow Carlitos to testify via videotape, but first he extracted a promise from Patrick that the child would be returned to his family just as soon as his health permits.

"That's always the fear in these cases," Patrick tells me. "There are already families in North Dakota asking if they can adopt him, and that's just in the short time since we contacted the hospital there."

Wouldn't he have a better life in the United States, I ask?

"Not necessarily," he answers. "His extended family is here and they love him. His heritage is here. He belongs here. You can't put too much emphasis on that. Also, Guatemalans consider their children to be their greatest treasure, and they don't like the idea of losing them to another country. To them, that's the same as giving up the future. And then there is the matter of the court case. The state has been looking to nail El

Pato for a long time, and they see this kid as their best chance. I shudder to think what might happen if the guy gets off," he adds.

All of this leads to a question about all of the children he's taken under his wing over the years. How, I wonder, could he have left the dozens of Guatemalan children he'd taken in all those years ago, first to work in Singapore, and then to go back to Bismarck?

"I didn't leave them," Patrick says with some heat. This is a sore subject, because Patrick knows that despite his best efforts, for a time he was unable to keep the children safe. He feels they were betrayed by the head of Casa Alianza just as he was, and one-by-one, they drifted back to the streets. "Before I left for Southeast Asia they were all in school and doing well," he says. "I checked up on them. I sent money and gifts regularly. I saw them when I could. When I left the agency I thought they were well. But I never turned my back on them." I remember his box of letters, those he wrote and those he received, and in them were dozens from the children, thanking him for his gifts and his cards.

BISMARCK, NORTH DAKOTA
Fall 1990

Patrick stared at the letter for a long time, then closed his eyes and laid his head down on the rickety table that a friend had donated for his apartment. He had come home late at night and found the dozen or so envelopes from Central America that the mailman had pushed under his front door. His new life, different as it was from his previous one, had brought a new peace, and he had finally managed to leave behind the world's slums, suffering children, prostitutes, human rights activism and the political maneuvering that had been his life for the past 10 years. Now, all of his time was being eaten up, either by his anonymous work at the asphalt plant or in fixing up his house.

But he could no longer ignore the children's letters. Lifting his head off the table once again, he looked down at a note from a boy who, with no warning or assistance, had been kicked out of the orphanage and had later attempted suicide.

"They just told me to put my things into a paper sack— then they drove me to the village where I was born and dropped me off on a street corner. They told me to go find a relative," the boy wrote. "You know, Patricio, that if I had a relative I wouldn't have been in that orphanage in the first place. The worst part is, I missed test day at school and now I'll have to take the entire school year over, if I ever do go back. Come back, Papa. We need you."

He checked the postmark and saw that it had taken weeks for the letter to reach him. He wondered where Walter and Enrique and Sonia and all of the other children who had written to him were now. His first reaction was worry. He knew from experience that even a few weeks on the streets could change a kid's life forever.

Four days later, Patrick faced his parents across the table in the same dining room where he had spent so many years as a child, explaining to them why he had to go back to Guatemala.

"But, Patrick, you just got home!" his mother said with real concern. It had been such a relief to have him back safe and sound. His work and travels to the world's most violent and dangerous points had worried her for years. And when he had stepped off the airplane this time, he had looked so sick and beaten down. He was only now beginning to get his health back. He was still wracked with malaria fevers that hit in waves every couple of weeks, and he was painfully thin.

"Mom, I can't just let those kids die on the streets. That's what will happen to them. They'll turn to prostitution or to doing or selling drugs. From there, they'll either be killed outright or end up in a hell-hole of a prison. I need to go back and see that they're safe."

"So this is temporary then?" his father asked.

"Yes, just a visit. Just long enough to find them a school and a foster home, so that at least they'll have a chance. I can't really explain it, but I know this is something God wants me to do."

"But you can't single-handedly save the world," his mother said. The last 10 years had taken a lot out of Patrick, physically and emotionally. Anybody could see it.

"Did I ever tell you about Jacinto?" he asked. "I know you've heard me mention him, but did I ever tell you how we really met?" They shook their heads. "He was about 12, I think," Patrick continued. "He was one of the smartest boys I have ever known, and he had the quickest sense of humor, too. We used to meet on the street and he'd entertain me for a while with jokes and these crazy stories that we both knew he was making up as he went along.

"But every once in a while, I'd get some small bit of truth out of him. Like the day he admitted that what he really wanted to do with his life was to become a teacher. He'd never told anybody that before because he knew that he didn't stand a chance of making that dream come true. This kid never knew his father, and I doubt his mother even knew who the guy was. She used to work the streets, do drugs. More than once she brought home men who went after Jacinto, and he had the scars to prove it. He spent most of his time living on the streets just to avoid them.

"I thought I could help him. I spent months being nice to him, buying him Cokes and ice cream, bringing him sandwiches, just trying to earn his trust. Finally, after all of that, I convinced him to take his chances with me. I brought him into the shelter, and got him off the streets, away from his mother." Patrick took a moment to remember how small and scared Jacinto had been, how tough he had acted. Bravado was his only weapon back then.

"Like a lot of the kids," he continued, "he had trouble settling down. He had nightmares—sometimes he would disappear for days and refuse to say where he had gone. When he was 15 he ran away from the orphanage for some silly reason. I think maybe he had a fight with one of the other boys. I never really did find out exactly what happened. But after he left he couldn't keep up with his schoolwork and he dropped out.

"I never saw him around anymore after that, although I heard the street talk about him. I eventually found him again after one of our social workers saw him hanging around a cheap hotel in Guatemala City. I sat in my car and waited for him to come out, and finally spotted him soliciting business outside this dump of a place near the airport. He was cold and hungry, painfully skinny and very dirty. His eyes looked sick. He was still extremely smart, which in his case made it worse because he knew he was slowly dying. I tried like the devil to get that boy back.

"Then one night in December, not long before I left for Southeast Asia, I got a phone call from Jacinto's brother saying that Jacinto was sitting on a bridge just outside of Guatemala City. He had gotten into a fight with some gang members, and was cut with a knife. There was some question about the injury. Some suggested that he had actually cut himself. When I got to him he was sitting on the ledge of a 180-foot high bridge, just sitting there, gazing into the empty space below him, crying like you can't believe."

Patrick stopped talking for a moment and took a sip of water. He was thinking about the look on Jacinto's face when he had crawled out onto that 180-foot ledge with him, and sat down beside him.

"I crawled out to him and we talked for a long time," Patrick continued. "Just sitting there on that narrow, cold ledge. I told him he was loved, that we could find a good home for him even after everything he had done, and that I would somehow put him through school if he would put in some effort—open a book now and then. I told him he could still have his dream of being a teacher if he really wanted it. He gave me this really intense sort of look, as if he were trying to read in my face whether I was handing him a line or not. Finally, he stood up and just said, 'OK,' and we left the bridge and walked home."

Patrick looked at his mother. "Now do you understand why I have to go back?" he asked. "When I walked him off that bridge ledge, we were 18 stories in the air, over a ravine. If he goes back there again, I know he's never going to come off of it alive."

Within days he was on a plane, heading south.

CHAPTER ELEVEN

Letter to a Friend

September 2, 1990

Dear Jim,

I continue to receive a flood of letters from Guatemala. Hard as I have tried to leave all of that behind, it seems that this situation is simply not going to let me go. The number of boys and girls for whom I am now responsible has grown to 18... this means that I pay for all of their housing, education, medical and living costs.

I don't see how I can do this from here in Bismarck. In a big way I really believed in our philosophy that these kids were our kids, and I don't think they should be abandoned now when they need us most.

I have to go back.

It amazes me to watch Patrick multi-task. As he works to save Carlitos, he is also busy running the programs that feed, clothe and care for thousands of people. His phone never stops ringing, and he passes out advice and solves problems for the steady line of people who always wait outside his office. But he also knows when it's time to take a break. He suggests dinner for me and for KFYR-TV photographer Dwayne Walker, who has joined me on this trip to Antigua. Patrick says he knows just the place.

Antigua, Guatemala, is a tourist mecca. It is beautiful, with its pastel, Spanish-style architecture and its streets paved in cobblestones. The houses front narrow sidewalks, with doors that open onto tiled courtyards planted with tropical flowers, broad-leaf plants and bubbling fountains. Many hotels are four-star, and the restaurants are excellent.

Outside the nightclubs, with doormen-slash-bouncers dressed in black suits and shiny shoes, you'll find foreign luxury cars of every make, limousines and sports cars. You can't help but notice them and their owners, beautiful men and women who leave them at the curb before joining the nightlife. What you may not notice right away, are the small boys who lurk in the shadows of the clubs and restaurants. I do not see them until one of them blocks our path and with a winning smile, offers to watch our car, which Patrick has already locked up with a variety of anti-theft devices for the steering column, the tires and the gas tank. Without hesitation, though, Patrick reaches into his pocket for a quetzal, which he hands over with a few words and a stern look.

"What did you tell him?" I ask as we enter the restaurant. This is one of his favorite eating establishments because the food here is reminiscent of what he would find at home. The menu offers pot roast and pork chops. He brings tourists here because his guests rarely complain afterwards that the food made them sick. Patrick, if pressed, will tell you that stomach complaints are almost inevitable after the first few days in any Central American country, because the bacteria in subtropical climates are so unlike what they would find in their own countries, but he says most stomachaches are minor and pass quickly. If he makes too much of it, he says, his guests become paranoid, are afraid to eat and feel worse for it.

"I have the best of both worlds," he told me when we're making the decision on where to eat that night. "I get sick here quite often...and I get sick my first few days back in Bismarck, too. My stomach never knows what to make of the situation."

As for the boy on the sidewalk, Patrick says, "I told him I haven't seen him at school. He's one of the boys in our elementary school at the Dreamer Center and he's been missing lately. I told him to come back."

"What about the money you gave him?"

"To watch the car. If I don't give the car-watchers money, I'll end up with some kind of damage. Scratched paint, broken mirror, something like that."

"But that's extortion!"

"Absolutely. I look at it as free enterprise. He figures if I can eat here, I can afford it." We go inside. That he can afford to eat here on this night is not something he takes for granted. Being broke is a condition that he's learned to live with. Not knowing where the next meal is coming from has at some times been a way of life. He tells me I would not believe some of the things he's done just to put food on the table, and he begins another story.

ANTIGUA, GUATEMALA
April 21, 1991

When Patrick stepped off the plane in Guatemala City there was very little fanfare, but there was somebody there to meet him. He had written to a former benefactor, a man who liked and admired him, explaining all that had happened, and asking for help. The man said he would help by giving Patrick free use of a long-abandoned farmhouse and car.

"They aren't much," the man had warned. Patrick had replied that he didn't need much, but he was still surprised when a stranger approached him at the gate, told him to follow him outside, and handed him the keys to the promised vehicle and a map to the benefactor's *finca*, or farm.

"It's parked over there," the man said. "I'll show you where it is, then you're on your own," he added with a quick smile.

Exiting the international airport terminal in Guatemala City, the stranger pointed to a paneled station wagon parked illegally right outside the main doors. At first Patrick could not believe what he was seeing. He wasn't picky, but this was beyond description. The car had no back or side windows. The glass had been replaced by sheets of tin painted black. The floorboards had so much rust that when Patrick opened the door and looked down, he could actually see the street between the car seats and down by the brake pedal. And there was a terrible smell.

"What was it used for?" he shouted at the man's retreating back.

"It was a pig truck. The farmer hauled pigs to market in the back of that thing. Good luck, my friend," he said with barely a backward glance.

Patrick looked at the stained floor of the station wagon with distaste, but noted that at least whatever was there was dry. Shrugging, he tossed his luggage into the back and climbed in. When he put the key in the ignition, the engine turned over right away, and he pulled away from the curb. A block later, as he rounded a corner leaving the airport, the car quit, and would not start again.

"Swell," he said to himself, before climbing out and leaning against the side of the old farm vehicle to wait for a passing taxi or tow-truck, knowing that to walk for help meant abandoning his suitcases to the first thief or street gang to come along. While considering his options, he bumped a piece of siding over the front wheel-well, which immediately broke loose and swung down, striking him in the side of the leg.

"Oh great!" Patrick cried out. "Welcome back to Guatemala, Patrick. What else can possibly happen now?"

As if in response, he heard thunder and within a few minutes, large drops of rain splashed onto the ground around him.

Twenty minutes later, a tow truck passed by, and a now-drenched Patrick was able to flag the driver down. The man driving it had brought along his entire family, which meant that there was no room in the cab of the truck for Patrick. There was nothing else to do but climb into the back of the pig truck. As soon as the front end of the truck was hoisted into the air, though, he turned around and watched as his luggage tumbled down and out through a broken tailgate. Banging on the side of the vehicle and shouting for the tow truck operator to stop, he reloaded the pig truck and then climbed inside after his luggage, this time getting a firm grip.

Anyone watching from a nearby sidewalk would have been amazed to see Patrick sitting in the back of that windowless, tin-covered converted station-wagon, riding at a 45-degree angle behind the tow truck's crane, grasping the back of the front seat with one hand and holding his luggage with the other. He pleaded to God for salvation and at the same time, hung on for dear life, just managing to keep his luggage from tumbling out of the pig-truck and onto the road a second time.

But the man did agree to give him a lift all the way to the farmhouse, which turned out to be a very long 90-minute ride from the airport. His clothes were a filthy mess, his arms were aching and his head pounding after the first bumpy mile, but he kept reminding himself that at least he wasn't walking, dragging his luggage behind him with a rope.

After dropping the pig-truck in front of a repair shop, the

tow truck operator and his family drove Patrick to his new home on the outskirts of the Caqchiquel Indian village of Pastores, about 10 minutes north of Antigua. He saw right away that he had his work cut out for him.

The benefactor had said that the caretakers were expecting him, and that much was true, but they weren't happy to see him and had made no accommodations for his visit. The caretakers lived in a small house on the property, but the large farmhouse was abandoned, overgrown with weeds and overrun by scorpions. Doors had rotted open, small animals had invaded the interior and a thick layer of dust covered everything.

"Well, uh, thanks," he said to the woman who begrudgingly showed him inside. She nodded irritably, handed Patrick a lit candle, and stalked out. It was clear that the owner had not been around to visit in quite some time and that this woman, Theresa, did not appreciate having her privacy or her routine disrupted.

Patrick sighed, went in and took a closer look.

The farmhouse itself was made of adobe, with thick walls and rotting wood floors. It was built in the shape of a "C" around a central courtyard. The rooms were large, and while there didn't appear to be any heat or electricity at the moment, there was a large, centrally-located fireplace. Patrick's bed was right where Theresa had said it would be, but the sheets and mattress had long ago become home to mice and bugs. Clearly, the first order of business was to look for wood and start a fire to chase the

Village of Nebaj, Qui-ch'e, a scene of frequent and violent bloodshed during Guatemala's civil war. 1983 Photo: Patrick Atkinson
Inset photo: Atkinson discovers a clandestine cemetery while excavating newly purchased property. Its discovery nearly leads to his murder. 1989 Photo: J. Evan Beauchamp

Atkinson receives Guatemalan National Congressional Medal for service to the poor of Guatemala, particularly women and the Mayan Indians both during and after the war.
2005 Photo: Miguel Angel Alvarez

1

Guatemala's 37-year civil war uprooted entire communities and vast numbers of rural farm families fled to the safety of the nation's capital, Guatemala City. Resulting poverty, violence, unemployment and alcoholism left many children alone in the streets. Atkinson founded Guatemala's first professional program to deal with this burgeoning street child population. Photos (top) Patrick Atkinson, 1986; (middle) Jena Gullo, 1996; (bottom) Chris Wadelton, 2004.

2

Counter clockwise starting at top left: Former street child and now physician Luis Enrique Perez with gunshot victim Carlitos Chuy; Luis Enrique Perez working in Atkinson's orphanage bread shop; Luis Enrique Perez in early adolescence. Photos: Patrick Atkinson *Top right: Atkinson welcoming Carlitos back to Guatemala after life-saving surgery in Bismarck, N.D.* Photo: Miguel Angel Alvarez

Students at the Rotary International School, Dreamer Center, Antigua, Guatemala.
2004 Photo: Patrick Atkinson

3

Counter clockwise starting top left: Homeless child living under a bridge in Tegucigalpa, Honduras, 1986; Street Child, Antigua, Guatemala, 1987; Homeless orphan living in Smokey Mountain garbage dump of Manila, Philippines, 1989 Photos: Patrick Atkinson
Center right: Homeless child's first day in Atkinson's new program in Guazapa, El Salvador, 2005 Photo: Jena Gullo
Top right: Atkinson worked to reunite war orphans with their families from 1987 until 1995. This child was tossed into a canyon by combatants and left for dead. Photo: J. Evan Beauchamp

After receiving hundreds of letters from Guatemalan children and former staff members, Atkinson made the decision to return to Guatemala to establish what would become The GOD'S CHILD Project. Top photo: Atkinson holds an abandoned boy at a GOD'S CHILD Project-assisted Guatemalan center for malnourished children, 2004. Photo: Pete Miller
Bottom photo: Atkinson hands out monthly scholarship checks and letters from sponsors at the Manchen "little house at the top of the hill" program site, 1992. Photo: Doc Mueller

Atkinson cancelled a stateside speaking tour and immediately returned to Guatemala to direct relief efforts when Hurricane Stan devastated the countryside. GOD'S CHILD Project volunteers and staff were later recognized for saving the lives of hundreds, and providing continued care and support for government relief efforts after other groups had left, 2005. Photo: Miguel Angel Alvarez

Atkinson translates for the author as she conducts an interview for a news series on the work of The GOD'S CHILD Project in one of Guatamala's prisons.
Photo: Bernardo Hernandez

In the late 1990s, Atkinson was asked by the United Nations to provide management training in East and South Africa. In 2001, he began health, education, and community development programs in Malawi, Africa, where malnutrition, disease and leprosy have devastated children's lives.

Photos: Miguel Angel Alvarez

7

Top photo: Atkinson with children at the project's Guatemala-based Dreamer Center.
2005 Photo: El Periodico
Bottom photo: Atkinson receives the Guatemalan National Congressional Medal from
Guatemalan Congressman Leonel Rodriguez, August 2005.
Photo: Miguel Angel Alvarez

chill from the room. It was already late, and pitch black, thanks to the overcast sky, the overhanging trees and the shadows of the mountains surrounding the farmhouse.

Patrick cleared a nest out of the chimney with a broom that he found leaning in a corner. After searching for another ten minutes, he found enough kindling to light the fire and, before long it was crackling merrily.

The firelight was also enough for him to see even more scorpions scuttling up the walls in his bedroom. There were spider webs dangling from the ceiling in every corner. The bed itself was infested with bugs as well as mice, but he was too tired to walk the 45-minute trip back into Antigua to find a clean hotel room. Patrick pulled the covers and sheets off and carried them out to the yard. He gave them a good shake, put them back on the bed, and tried not to think about anything at all as he climbed in, rolled his jacket into a pillow, and out of sheer exhaustion, fell asleep. He ignored what crawled over him during the night.

In the morning he rolled up his sleeves and set to work. With a broom and water, he began to scrub. He saw little of the caretakers, although every once in a while he'd spot one of them standing on the edge of a nearby coffee field, watching him out of the corner of an eye. In small ways, they continued to let him know that they didn't want him there.

Much of that first morning was spent cleaning his bedroom and washing the bedding. Then he started on the main living room and the dining room, then the bathrooms. At the end of that first day he was physically exhausted, but he needed his pig truck, his only transportation, so he set out walking the narrow, busy road that led from the farm into Antigua.

Arriving in Antigua nearly an hour later, Patrick walked down the main business street toward the car repair shop where the pig truck had been dropped the night before. Along the way, he spotted Lorenzo Sipac, who had been one of the small, frightened Mayan Indian children whom Patrick had rescued from the war-devastated village of Chipiacul, Chimaltenango, almost eight years ago to the day. Lorenzo had just turned 18, and Patrick could not believe how happy he was to see him. All day he had felt isolated, and now, walking down the main street, people whom he had known for years treated him coldly. He had never felt more alone.

"Lorenzo!" he called out as he saw the young man approach. "Hey, Lorenzo. How's life going?"

"Patricio! What are you doing here? We heard you were still in the United States."

"I kept getting letters from the kids, saying they were on the streets and in trouble and asking me to come back, so here I am."

"Well, welcome back, Patricio. The world hasn't been the same since you left. It's been crazy—really, really crazy. So... what do you think about all the rumors flying around about you?"

"What rumors? I haven't heard much yet," Patrick said. "Then again, I just got here late last night."

"All kinds of strange things. Do you remember that stone platform we built in the scrub brush out in the field behind the big house? How we'd all go out there for campfires and sit around singing songs and telling ghost stories? Well, apparently one of the Casa Alianza doctors told one of the local clergy that you used to hold black masses there."

Patrick was momentarily speechless. "That's crazy," he finally said.

Lorenzo nodded. "I know. I know, but these are crazy times."

Patrick felt like crying as Lorenzo told him more and more stories that had been floated about him while he had been gone, but at least now he knew what he was up against. There was nothing for him to do about it now except to make sure he remained in plain view so that people would see how ridiculous those stories were.

"So, where are you staying?" he asked Lorenzo.

"Oh, here and there. No place permanent. Depends on where I'm working."

"If you need a place, I have an old farmhouse that I'm staying in for now. It has four bedrooms, if you want to call them that, and I sure could use the company. To be honest, it's way too quiet and dark out there. I think the caretaker's wife hates me, and the place is crawling with scorpions."

"Sounds like an offer I can't refuse," Lorenzo said with a laugh. He then leaned across and gave Patrick a big hug. "Welcome back viejo, old man. You can't imagine how much we've missed you."

That night, Lorenzo moved into the abandoned farmhouse on the outskirts of Antigua, and like Patrick the night before, he took great care to shake the mouse droppings out of the sheets, promising to buy bleach and "tons and tons" of soap the next day.

Word spread quickly that Patrick was back in Guatemala. While some people eyed him warily, others ran into the streets to greet him. They remembered that he had cared for them and that life with him had been good. He didn't need to look for the children that he had come home to save. They found him. He woke up the next morning to find Javier Alvarado sitting outside on the steps, enjoying the warm morning sun while waiting for Patrick to leave his room.

The following day there were two more, and then a half a dozen more the day after that. By week's end, he had 18 kids coming by, looking for a safe place inside, off the streets. Some had been living in small rooms in Antigua and in the surrounding villages, while others had been sleeping outside under park benches or in doorways surrounding Central Park. The homeless ones were offered the other spare bedrooms in the farmhouse, and when those were full, they were told they could lie down for the night wherever they found a dry, flat place.

"They can't all stay here," Patrick told Lorenzo after that first week. "We'll have to find foster families for them or something, and definitely get to work on getting them back into school."

"That's going to take money," Lorenzo said, "and from what I've seen so far, you didn't bring too much of that with you."

Before leaving North Dakota, Patrick had sold almost all of his personal possessions and had accumulated about $11,000. To get the children who now flocked to him back into school he had to clean them up, find a doctor to clear them of the parasites and diseases they had acquired in their months on the streets, and buy school supplies for them. If they had no place to stay, and most of them didn't, he would also have to pay foster families for their care.

Then there were the walk-ins—the friends of the children he had come back to find, who also wanted to get in off the streets.

Frequently, he'd hear that a child had joined a street gang or that a girl had gone to work in a local house of prostitution, just to stay alive. Once the child belonged to a gang or moved into a cantina, Patrick knew, the gang leaders and the bar owners virtually owned them, and the only way he could get them out was to buy their freedom. That, too, was going to take money, in addition to nerves and more trips into the nation's worst slums.

Dreading the work that lay ahead of him if these children

were going to survive, Patrick began to take long walks so that he could be alone to pray, listen to God, and think about what he was supposed to do now. Finding no answers one day, he climbed a nearby mountainside with Lorenzo and told him that he didn't think he had the strength to do this work again.

"I'm terrified, Lorenzo," Patrick confided. "I'm broke and not connected anymore. My God, just 15 months ago I was rubbing elbows and discussing childcare issues with some pretty highly-placed people, and now I can't even feed all of you dinner tonight. I don't know what's happening because I shouldn't even be here right now. I've already put in my time and worked too many years in these ditches."

Lorenzo listened to his "old man," and after a few minutes, said, "Do you remember how you raised us, Patrick? How you always told us to do the best that we could, because God only cares that we try our best to do what is right? These kids are dying, Patrick. Even if we all die tomorrow, at least we'll die knowing that you loved us enough to come back and give it your best try. But we're not going to die. God is doing something here, I can promise you that."

Heartened by Lorenzo's faith, Patrick turned back to his work. He cared for his growing family with little more than prayers and scraps. By being creative with the many 'old family recipes' he invented with whatever was on hand, they almost always had enough to eat, even when the guest list grew by a dozen.

Soon enough he learned to go into a·fast food restaurant whenever he saw one and order a few hamburgers and fries, and to always ask for lots and lots of ketchup packets. He asked for ketchup even if he only ordered a soda, or even just water. Patrick then took the hamburger, fries, and ketchup home and cut everything up into small pieces—bun, pickles and the lettuce. To this he added the extra ketchup and water, and sometimes rice if there was any. He called it Big Mac Soup and the kids ate it without complaint. He told them it was an old recipe, one that had been in his family for seven generations. They didn't know whether to believe him, of course, but they always smiled and held out their bowls. If a new child showed up at the door while the group was eating, he simply excused himself from the table, added more water, ketchup and salt, and somehow there was always enough to feed everyone.

After visiting possible benefactors in Guatemala City one afternoon, he brought a ragtag bunch of boys and girls into a local McDonald's restaurant. The owner, Yolanda de Fernandez de Cofiño, spotted the group sitting at a table by the window, sharing their hamburgers and milk. There hadn't been enough money to buy something for everyone, so Patrick wasn't eating.

"Patrick! When did you get back to Guatemala?" the owner asked him. Patrick explained why he had returned and what he and the kids were doing. The woman noticed that there was no food in front of Patrick and that the others were sharing their drinks. She ordered the group to sit tight for a moment and went into her office. When she came out she beckoned Patrick over.

"Listen, let me give you this," she said. It was a card, good for free food at any McDonald's restaurant that she managed, anytime. "You have to eat. You'll be no good to these children if you starve to death. Also, I know you and the children didn't get enough to eat, so today's meal is on me." Calling over one of the counter employees, the owner told her to take everyone's order again. Seeing that one of the children, out of shame or out of shyness, had ordered very little, she said, "A growing girl like you can't live on so little food. Let's double that order!"

This was the first real kindness Patrick had experienced from the public since returning to Guatemala, and he was moved. It gave him hope for the future.

It was one thing to promise to care for the children and to get them back into school. Paying for it all, however, was something else. He had to personally raise the money to pay for their clothing, medical care, school supplies and living expenses. To do this, he accepted just about every kind of odd job imaginable—anything he was offered. He drove a truck, did manual labor, unloaded medicines and embassy supplies that arrived at the international airport, and gave tours to visiting tourists and dignitaries. He even accepted a job making television commercials after somebody from an agency saw him dancing with a lady friend in a nightclub one evening and liked his "international" look. Whatever he could do to bring in more money, he did.

"Amigo," a co-worker said to him one night as they unloaded boxes from the back of a truck, "you're looking pretty tired tonight. In fact, you always look tired."

"Too many jobs, not enough sleep," Patrick replied as he turned to lift another box. He was grateful that tonight they weren't too heavy. He was weary, there was no doubt about that, and his old back injuries were plaguing him. That morning he had done some concrete work, and in the afternoon he had driven several of the children to the clinic for treatment for their worms. He had been hoping for a couple of hours of uninterrupted sleep before morning, but that was before this latest job offer had come along.

"I've seen you with all those kids," the co-worker said. "They can't all be yours."

"They're not, by blood at least. God's asked me to raise them, so that's what I've got to do. Want a couple?" Patrick asked with a laugh, although it was clear what he expected the answer to be.

"Yeah, well, I'd say you have enough," the man replied with a chuckle, "and no thanks. I've got plenty of my own at home."

Patrick knew the man was right. It probably was time to draw the line. But it was hard to turn away hungry kids, especially when they had no place else to go. He remembered what his mother had said before he left, that he couldn't save the whole world.

Still, the conversation got him thinking about some of the fundraising methods that he'd seen other groups use successfully. First, he decided, he would teach himself to speak in public. Then, he thought, he would take the message of his newly founded organization on the road. After consulting with Fr. Tom Kramer, his parish priest and friend back in Bismarck, he decided to call it The GOD'S CHILD Project.

The next day, he borrowed an old, rickety typewriter, bought some plain white paper and cheap envelopes, and sat down to write his first newsletter appeal to friends and family back home. He knew that they would help.

While he waited for them to respond, he accepted into his program nearly all of the new children who came knocking, still trusting that God would somehow provide the necessary funds. He also taught the children to pray long and hard, and to trust what he told them, that God would inspire other people to help.

CHAPTER TWELVE

Fund-raising letter

October, 1991

Dear Friends,

The lights went out last night while nine of our children were folding and sealing my last letter to you. The whole room suddenly turned black and stayed that way until Alejandro returned with his six small candles. His light soon gave our adobe home a sense of glowing warmth, and the children went back to their licking and folding, and the sticking on of your stamps.

I went about my parental thing, setting up a battery lamp and tripping over a small girl sleeping on the floor. Before I turned the lamp on, however, I turned around and learned the eternal magic of candles. There was my legal son Miguel, sitting in the orange glow of a small candle and quietly closing your envelopes. He wasn't laughing like the others and seemed very lost in his thoughts. I wondered what they were, yet was afraid to ask. He's known some pretty terrible things in his few short years.

I first met Miguel on a park bench in Antigua's Central Park. I didn't know it at the time, but I was sitting in his living room.

In a small city like Bismarck, North Dakota, word travels fast. News of Carlitos' nightmare quickly turns into a media event that needs to be managed. Patrick begins receiving e-mails from reporters and soon realizes that the little boy's story is of great interest, not only to people at the hospitals, but to the community at large. The story seems to touch people's hearts in a remarkable way, and within days Bismarck residents are lining up to offer help of all kinds.

Before the details of the child's travel arrangements are even worked out, Patrick finds himself giving phone interviews. The media spotlight has never been a comfortable place for him, but he has learned to use it to the children's advantage. He recognizes that some stories touch people more than others, and inspire them to help.

Some people might see this as crass, but Patrick says it is simply reality. "People want to help," he insists. Make a specific request of someone on behalf of a child, and few with the ability to help will refuse to do so.

"Tell people that there is famine in Africa, they shake their heads and try not to think about it. It is simply too overwhelming," he explains. "Tell people about a child who needs a life-saving surgery, though, and the offers come pouring in.

"People are all heroes," he adds. "Just give them the chance and a story they can relate to." It's a secret to human nature that he has learned to tap into.

One of Patrick's most famous stories involves the boy, Miguel. This is not his real name. Patrick nearly always changes names when he writes about the children, to protect their privacy and their dignity. The experiences they have lived through are so terrible that in some ways their only hope of a normal life is to try to forget. This particular boy's story is so compelling, though, that the secret has been hard to keep. Even so, Patrick asks me not to name him.

"Just call him Miguel," he insists.

Antigua, Guatemala
CENTRAL AMERICA
1992

Patrick had watched the boy for days. Their paths crossed each morning as he walked his dog in the murky, early morning light. It seemed too early for a child that age to be up and about. He couldn't have been more than 10 years old, and he seemed to be alone. In fact, Patrick couldn't help but notice how the boy glanced around nervously, as if he were trying to avoid being spotted. The boy would wait until he thought Patrick and his dog had left Antigua's Central Park plaza before he walked noiselessly to the fountain in the middle of the square and washed, still glancing around him from time to time to be sure he had not been spotted. Patrick later saw him dash into some bushes on the side of the square, and when he emerged, he was dressed in school clothes and carrying schoolbooks.

"He's got to be homeless," Patrick thought to himself. "But he's in school. I wonder how he gets the money for his books." He received his answer several nights later when he opened his front door and saw the same boy standing there, dressed in ragged clothes again and carrying a shoeshine box.

"Shine?" he asked with an eager smile, nodding at Patrick's bare feet.

"Uh, OK, sure," he said. "But let me find some shoes first." He rooted around in his closet for the better part of five minutes before locating an old pair of dress shoes—the ones he wore with his only suit whenever he had to go to court to plead with a judge on behalf of one of his kids, an event that was becoming more and more frequent as their numbers grew.

Last month he had taken in 10 new children—this month 15. They were up to 43 already, and he was running out of room to house them. Word was spreading fast that kids could go to him for help or for food, and he was still having a tough time turning the hungry ones away. He certainly didn't need another mouth to feed. Yet, this kid in the park by the fountain seemed unique. He was homeless, and from all appearances, was putting himself through school. That kind of drive was rare in one so young and so obviously on his own. Patrick returned to the front door where the boy waited, and handed him the shoes.

As Miguel started shining, Patrick asked him a few

questions. The answers he received were cheerful enough, but contained no useful information. Yes, the boy was in school in the mornings. Where were his parents? That question earned Patrick a shrug and a smile. Where did he sleep? Another shrug, another smile and the boy handed back the shoes and held out his hand. Patrick dug into his pocket and located some quetzals, the local Guatemalan currency, which he handed over to the boy.

"See you around," he called after him. The boy nodded and was gone.

The next day, Patrick approached him in the square. It was late evening, just getting dark. The boy was sitting on a park bench eating a hotdog, which he'd purchased from a nearby vendor.

"How's business?" Patrick asked. The boy shrugged and began to move away. Since he'd been on his own he'd found that it was never a good idea to get too close to people he didn't know too well. Most of the adults he came into contact with considered him a nuisance at best, a target for abuse at worst. Either way, he knew that other people usually didn't want him around, unless he was there to work for the pennies that they threw his way.

The boy moved over and casually joined a larger group of boys standing on a nearby street corner. Safety in numbers was Miguel's philosophy, and the boys usually didn't mind his presence, so long as he kept his mouth shut. Patrick looked over at the group and recognized Julio, one of the boys whom he had briefly cared for years earlier.

"Patricio!" Julio cried in excited recognition. "I didn't know you were back."

"Yeah, for a while now," he said, then reached into his pocket and pulled out a handful of coins. "Anybody here want an ice cream?" he asked, and the boys clustered around him. He knew better than to hand them the cash. Instead, he walked them over to a nearby ice cream shop and bought them each a cone. He noticed that the shoeshine boy had come, too, though he was still hanging on the fringes of the group. How old was he? With street kids it could be tough to tell because they tended to be malnourished and small. Maybe eight? Maybe nine? Patrick turned away and started a conversation with the other boys, in a voice loud enough that the shoeshine boy would also be able to hear.

"You all look as if you're staying well fed," he said.

"Sure," replied Julio. "We get by."

With a quick glance, Patrick could tell that these kids were now members of a street gang, which in all likelihood meant that they were "getting by" picking pockets or selling drugs. Some of them were clearly using drugs, too, although they were probably going for the cheaper, hunger-killing high that could be found at the bottom of a half-filled baby food jar of shoe glue. He saw the telltale blush in one boy's cheeks, and the typical runny nose, red-rimmed eyes and distant, spaced-out expression.

"Yeah, I came back a couple of months ago because I heard that some of the kids needed help," Patrick said to Julio in a voice loud enough for everyone to hear. "And I started a small project. We're living in an old farmhouse outside of Pastores. It's not bad and at least it gets everyone off the streets and gives them a place to do their homework."

"That's cool, Patrick, but we don't need that. We're doing fine. But thanks," Julio said, although his tone lacked conviction. Patrick had thought for a minute that he might have gotten through to him, but he decided it wasn't the right time to push any points.

"Hey, we're the first farm to the right, just before you get into Pastores. The caretaker who sometimes watches the gate is a pain in the butt, but if you come out you shouldn't have any problems getting around him." As he walked away, he noticed the shoeshine boy slipping back into the shadows of the park, still eating his ice cream.

In the days that followed Patrick learned a lot about the boy, just by observing him from a distance while he walked his dogs. For instance, he now knew that he slept under the park benches, wrapped in newspapers. He piled leaves and trash around himself to escape notice. It usually worked, although twice Patrick had witnessed the boy fending off unwelcome advances—once by a street sweeper who started kicking him and calling him trash, and another time by a man who appeared to be offering him money for something. When the boy refused the money, the man had become menacing, so Patrick had walked up to them and asked the time. The man said he didn't have a watch and walked off. The boy didn't say a word. He ran from the square, and Patrick had no idea where he slept that night.

From what Patrick could see, Miguel's pattern was almost always the same. Each morning he rose at sunrise, washed in the public fountain, dressed in the bushes and stashed his shoeshine equipment and work clothes. Then, at midday, he'd return to the square, glance around to make sure he was alone, dash back into the bushes, change back into his work clothes and once again begin going door-to-door to shine shoes for people in their homes.

Patrick brought Miguel a blanket one day, which the boy hid in the bushes along with the rest of his belongings. He smiled his thanks, but said little. Patrick frequently brought food, too. When the weather turned colder he brought a jacket. Bit-by-bit, Miguel opened up.

He had been abandoned by his father, he said, and tossed out by his mother at the age of 7 because she had a new husband who didn't want him. He had been on the streets ever since, almost two years now. Patrick admired his grit and determination, but also knew that he was a kid who didn't know how to trust. Too many bad things had happened to Miguel, and he had decided that it wasn't worth it to trust people. His chances were better on his own. Patrick accepted that, and simply helped out whenever he could.

One day, Miguel wasn't in the square. Patrick waited for several hours, didn't see him, and left. He tried not to dwell on it. After all, Miguel wasn't his kid, he told himself, and he already had plenty of children at home to worry about. At the same time, he knew what kinds of things happened to children on the streets. The week before he had read in the paper about a shop owner who had doused a huddle of sleeping children with gasoline and set them on fire. The man said he was tired of having "rats" cluttering up the sidewalk outside his shop.

And there were common illnesses, like diarrhea and pneumonia, which routinely killed street children. He hoped that little Miguel had not fallen victim to something or someone.

Several days later, Patrick heard a scuffle outside the farmhouse and looked outside to see what the commotion was about. And there was Miguel. The caretaker had him by the scruff of the neck and was marching him toward the outside gate. Patrick took off toward the door, but by the time he got outside there was no sign of Miguel. He must have scampered off into the coffee fields.

"What happened?" he asked.

"Some kid. He says he knows you," the caretaker said.

"He does. Where did he go?" Patrick asked.

"I don't know. I didn't think you'd want him around. He smelled like a sewer and he had marks all over his face and arms. I think he's sick. I told him to get lost."

"I've been trying to get him to come here for weeks," Patrick said in exasperation. "Look, if you see him again, don't talk to him, just tell me." He hated to think of a sick little boy sleeping out in the field all night or heading back into the streets because this guy had scared him off.

But that night, Miguel slipped past the caretaker and got by Patrick's dogs. He had waited, hidden in the fields until he saw the lights go off. He then guessed which window belonged to Patrick's room, because it was the last room to settle into darkness. He sat outside that window for the rest of the night, wrapping his arms around his skinny legs to ward off the chilly mountain air, until he heard Patrick's alarm ring at 5:30 the next morning. Then he rapped on the window.

Patrick moaned, pulled the blanket over his head, but then decided to check it out. He crawled out of bed and opened the door, but he saw no one there. When he heard the rapping again, he peered out the window and recognized Miguel, obviously tired and cold, and much the worse for wear.

"What happened to you?" he asked, opening the window and telling the boy to come closer so they wouldn't have to shout. The caretaker was right—he did smell awful.

"I was going door-to-door shining shoes like I always do," Miguel said in a tired voice, "and at one house, the boy who answered the door was one of my classmates. He recognized me and started to laugh. Then he told the others at school that I live on the street and shine shoes. The next night some boys from my class came around and beat me up, stole my shoeshine box, and threw my books into the fountain in the park. I climbed in to get the books back, but the cops came and made me get out. When I told them what had happened, they laughed, took my books away and said I probably didn't even know how to read. As they walked away I saw one of the cops tearing out the pages, one by one. Now everything is ruined."

As the boy finished telling his tale, tears started tracking down through the dirt on his face and this time he didn't even bother to wipe them away. He saw the loss of his books as the end of his dream to be something better. He couldn't afford to buy new ones, and anyway, without his books the teachers weren't going to allow him to go to class.

It had taken him a couple of days, but he had managed to track Patrick down. Finally, he was ready for help.

Patrick told Miguel to go around to the front door, and he let him in, then woke Lorenzo to help clean him up and get him something to eat. Once he saw to the boy's immediate needs, Patrick climbed into his pig truck and headed into town to see a lawyer friend.

Later that day, armed with legal advice, Patrick took Miguel to a judge to ask for temporary custody. That granted, the next order of business was to get the young boy some medical care. He had parasites under his skin, his teeth were bad, and he had a serious eye infection. Once care was initiated, Miguel joined Patrick's growing family. The very next day, he was back in school. His clothes were new, as were his books and even his shoes. No one doubted him now when he denied that he lived in the streets.

Life was literally a hand-to-mouth operation in the early days of The GOD'S CHILD Project. Patrick was working 115 hours a week to keep the kids clothed, fed and in school. He was running the project like an extended family, and his was the only wallet. By the summer of 1991 all of the money that he had brought with him was gone, and as hard as Patrick worked, the bills were piling up. The tuition was overdue, two of the children had come in so sick that they were in the hospital, and the entire group had been eating Big Mac Soup for days. Even with the few donations he was receiving from friends in the States, Patrick was broke.

He told Lorenzo, "I've tried everything I can, and I just can't work any harder. I've been praying to God to help us, but we're not going to make it. I mean, look!" he said holding up $11,000 in unpaid bills he had laid out on a table in front of him. For a man who unloads trucks for $20 a day, that was a lot of money. "It just isn't going to work," he said.

Patrick began his first week that month looking for other charities willing to take over the responsibility of raising and educating the children he had tried to support. The trouble was no one wanted to take in 14- and 15-year-old adolescents, since most groups preferred to work with much younger children.

Lorenzo and a few of the other children who had known

Patrick for years were also becoming concerned about his health. He was very often sick, and he was much too thin. One particularly bad battle with hepatitis and pneumonia had dropped his weight from 155 lbs. down to 108 lbs. The kids were also beginning to wonder what was going to happen to them.

"God has brought us this far," Patrick told them. "He isn't going to abandon us now, though I don't know how this is supposed to end. But you'll be taken care of," he assured them.

Several evenings later, Patrick was sitting alone at the dining room table at the farm, sorting through the bills that had to be paid immediately from those that could wait, when he heard a loud knock on the outside door. It was Kathy, an old friend from Mandan, North Dakota, who had come down to visit Guatemala.

"Come on in," Patrick said, happy to have his attention distracted from the financial mess that lay before him. "Let's see what I can get for you to eat."

Over reheated vegetable soup, the two friends shared stories about what was happening back in their hometowns, and what new developments there were in Guatemala. Kathy had been traveling around the countryside for several days now, visiting Indian villages up in the Highlands, the mountainous terrain that lay just across a river from the southern Mexican border.

"Well," Kathy said after a long, thoughtful pause, "maybe you can help me out with something. Remember Fr. Charlie

Backes? Before I left Mandan, Fr. Backes gave me a donation that he asked me to give to others who I thought might need some help. He specifically asked me to visit you and to see how you were doing."

There was another long pause, and then Kathy continued, "During this trip I've seen a lot of projects that need help, but either I wasn't carrying the money with me at the time, or else they didn't have any way to change it from US dollars to Guatemalan quetzals. Now, here's the problem. I'm heading back to the States tomorrow, and I still haven't given away most of Father's donation, so I'm going to leave it with you. I know that he'll be happy that I'm doing this. All he asks is that you pray for him."

The amount she gave to Patrick that night was $12,000. After paying the bills that had been laid out before him, there was still $1,000 left over to see the children through the rest of the month.

After Kathy left to return to Antigua later that night, Patrick woke up Lorenzo and several of the other children, and together they took the small flashlight up into the mountains behind the farmhouse. Patrick first laughed as he told the group what had happened, and then he shook his head in amazement. He knew that God had sent a messenger to let him know the answer that they had been searching for; everything was going to work out just fine, if only they would work hard, and trust that He wasn't ever going to let them down. But they were outgrowing the farm. Patrick had thought of expanding, perhaps moving some of the children into the outbuildings, but they were ramshackle and he couldn't be sure they would be safe.

Guatemala's 37-year-old civil war was winding down, but the violence didn't stop overnight. At the farmhouse on the road to Pastores, there were always strangers passing through, usually at night and in silence. They caused no commotion but even so, Patrick and Lorenzo were beginning to get a bad feeling about the place. While they had been at the farm, it had been a good home for them and for the children. They had cleaned up the land and rebuilt the buildings, and over time had cared for more than 70 children there.

In the spring of 1992 Lorenzo was cleaning out an abandoned storehouse on the farm, when he uncovered stacks of bloodstained mattresses. He felt his skin crawl, and together with the boys who had been helping him, backed out of the storehouse. He called Patrick over. Patrick took one look, before going inside to get a camera. He took pictures of the bloodstained mattresses, and then took the photos to the owner of the farm, who claimed he knew nothing about it. By the time Patrick returned to the farmhouse, though, the mattresses had been burned. There was no trace of them.

A short time later the entire group was walking along a creek that ran down the mountainside behind the farm, when they came across a large puddle of fresh blood pooled on a flat stone in the middle of the creek. Patrick wasn't sure what had happened, but he began to suspect that rebel guerillas were using at least part of the farm. He also wondered if part of the land was not being used for some other illegal purpose. Regardless, he was no longer comfortable living there and knew it was time to begin the search for a new place to live and run the project. Within a few days, they found and rented a small, yellow, two-room house at the top of a hillside footpath, in a neighborhood called El Manchen. The fledgling, yet quickly growing GOD'S CHILD Project moved into this home during Holy Week of 1992, and the program was run from there for the next six years.

Later that same year, a piece of land along a mostly dried up river called El Pensativo came up for sale. Patrick decided to buy the land and with the help of volunteers, build a new center there. But before it could even be finished, the project had outgrown this property. In 1996, the search began yet again for a larger home.

This time Patrick found a site that had been the former municipal garbage dump for the neighborhood of San Felipe de Jesus, located right at the base of the San Felipe slums.

With an unwavering faith that God was with him, and with the help of volunteers from around the world, he began to build once again.

CHAPTER THIRTEEN

A letter from Patrick Atkinson to Erma Bombeck

Dear Erma,

I am writing to say thanks for making life easier to live.

Who else but you understands that kids really can hear the fizz of the last bottle of Pepsi from 500 meters? Could anybody else have taught me to forgive the five-year-old who emptied a canister of dog repellant tear gas in my bedroom? At 10:00 at night, after a horrible day? And to hug him afterwards so that he doesn't feel bad, even telling him that it might kill the flies? It is often hard to continue here in Guatemala, and the loneliness and separation from family and friends can sometimes confuse the basic beliefs in service and Christ's love. Your books, however, continually add that necessary spark which keeps my vocation alive. In your own way, you point out the beauty of the "little" joys in life.

I mean, I really think you understand that the 13-year-old meant well when he gave me a homemade spring-loaded bug swatter for my birthday. And that there really is beauty within each of the 125 watermelon seed-coated, 10 pound-can-turned-flower-vases that I receive each Father's Day. And I know that it came from the heart when the three-year-old gave me a soft kiss and whispered "Happy Mother's Day" in my ear last year.

Most of the children I'm caring for here were orphaned in the country's violent civil war or abandoned to survive in its streets. Many of them arrive very damaged, and some are simply not going to make it.

At times, I feel myself trying to build an emotional wall with a newer kid if he is dying because I know that it will be a painful relationship, and I don't know if I have that much strength left. Just when it seems that I need the encouragement the most, however, you remind me that these children are priceless gifts from God. They are innocent kids whose fates were drawn and not chosen, and whose lives should end with balloons and belly-rubs rather than bullets and hunger.

I think that you understand without explanation that children can be separated into three age groups—those who go through my garbage, those who go through my desk, and those who go through my clothes and my car.

I also believe that you know the value of the brotherhood that forms when eight teen-aged boys crowd into a two-door, sub-compact car to listen to the radio, even though the very same music is playing in the rec room.

In many ways, you've taught me to be forgiving. I thought of you when a group of seven-year-old boys played hide-and-seek under the Archbishop's robes…while the Archbishop was still in them. And you were in my mind when 15 cheering boys brought me a field rat they had just trapped and killed near the pigpens, while I was showing the project to the nation's First Lady.

Finally, I am beginning to accept that I will never again know the beauty of a white shirt.

I no longer forgive a lot of kids because of you. It's not that I've become hard and cold. Rather, it's because you have shown me that they have done nothing wrong that needs forgiving, and with their little bumblings, they have certainly done a whole lot right.

Every day has been a challenge, and there are many days after which I want to return home and begin my own life.

But something bigger is happening here. It has a design that could only have been born from God's divine sense of humor and compassion. I don't know what it is, but I thank God every day for showing me bits and pieces of it.

And thank YOU for being such a tremendous source of strength, laughter and renewal. Your insights have helped me to remember with a smile some really rough days, and some good ones too, like the ones in which Carlos learned to walk, Menchi to count or Jorge to drive a car. If it was a downright terrible day, then maybe I will one more time be reminded of why I am never going to buy a white shirt again.

Sincerely,
Patrick Atkinson

Dear Pat,
I cannot believe that I have done all of that for you. You do yourself a great disservice. It takes a very special person to hang in there...whether you have one child or 508 of them.

I'll savor your letter and on days when I hear from religious fanatics who want to save my soul or someone who thinks I'm being too irreverent, I will re-read it and know that somebody out there likes me.

You remind me a lot of my son, who is also a teacher.   He taught in American Samoa and was also in the Peace Corps in Liberia.   It is a lonely business.

I'm taking a chance that you have not read my latest effort. Please accept it with love and appreciation.

Regards,
Erma Bombeck

I take the book from Patrick's hand and we both smile at the title. *"You Know It's Time To Go Home When You Look Like Your Passport Photo,"* he reads out loud. "Sure, assuming you still *have* your passport."

He received the letter from humor writer, Erma Bombeck in 1989, and he keeps it framed in his office. He enjoys looking at it. I found his response to the letter in his basement box of correspondence. The title to the book reminds him of a story.

It seems that Oscar Adrian, one of the most challenging children in the project, one year grew tired of Patrick traveling so much, and set fire to Patrick's passport after he learned that you need a passport to leave the country.

"It was the most sincere expression of love I have ever

received," he tells me as we head into town to try yet again to expedite arrangements for Carlitos' visa to leave the country. "I keep reminding myself of how loved I am whenever I stand in long lines at the passport office," he adds, a handful of forms clutched in his fist. Two hours later Patrick leaves the building with a valid temporary travel visa for Carlitos. That's one more hurdle overcome. But there are still many others.

Patrick arranges a conference call to St. Alexius in Bismarck so that he can talk to the doctors there and answer their questions. Urologist Dr. Lewis Cunningham had reservations when he was first approached by Dr. Mickelson with details about the little boy.

"I'm glad to help," he says now, "but first I want to be reasonably certain I can fix the child's problem." What he doesn't want to do, he says, is put the boy through a long trip if his case is medically hopeless. Because Patrick wants to get Carlitos back to Guatemala fairly quickly, Dr. Cunningham also wants to be certain that the little boy is not in for multiple surgeries and that there's no unacceptable risk of infection that would keep him hospitalized longer than expected.

Dr. Cunningham scans the reports that Patrick had faxed to him earlier and spots a problem.

"It says here that his catheter can't be removed. Why is that?"

Dr. Mickelson, who has spoken with The Dreamer Center doctor about Carlitos, says, "Apparently whenever they've tried to remove the catheter the urethra closes back up so they've just assumed that his injury is permanent."

"So the same dirty catheter has been sticking out of that little boy since the day he sustained the injury?" he asks. Dr. Mickelson says that's apparently the case. "Then that could be the cause of his low-grade fever," Dr. Cunningham adds.

The doctors agree that there could be other injuries involved, too, that they can't see without examining the boy themselves. But Dr. Cunningham feels confident enough in his ability to help Carlitos that he gives Patrick the go ahead.

"I'd say let's get the child up here and find out what's going on," he says before ending the call.

Moments later, Patrick heads out to his van. We are on our way to Jocotenango to tell cousin Luis the good news. In Carlitos' neighborhood, there are no phones, so messages have to be delivered in person.

The next order of business is to contact the airline and try to use frequent flyer miles on a moment's notice. Never easy, but the story is compelling. Patrick believes in his powers of persuasion, because he believes they come from a higher source.

"It's always amazing to me the direction that help will come," he says. Often when he leasts expects it.   He smiles. "Did I ever tell you how we got this van you're sitting in?"

ANTIGUA, GUATEMALA
1992

Patrick was running late. He had an appointment to meet a Hollywood movie star, and just before he climbed into the project's infamous pig truck to go, he noticed that both of its front tires were flat. The truck had been ancient when he'd taken his first drive in it, heading away from the airport on his first day back in Guatemala, so mechanical problems were a way of life—but still, he was frustrated at the timing of the flat tires. He considered changing the tires, but he had only one spare that was usable, and besides, there simply wasn't time. With a heavy sigh, he left a note for Lorenzo to see about getting new tires for the truck, then hopped on his bicycle and peddled the seven miles into town.

Patrick had never heard of the actor he was about to meet, but he knew that the man was famous for his involvement in the human rights movements of California and Central America. His name was Martin Sheen. Sheen was coming to visit and offer support to a number of programs in Guatemala and El Salvador. He had already stirred up publicity about the region's long history of human rights abuses—publicity which the country's governments were trying hard to downplay. Through a mutual friend, Sheen had heard about the work that The GOD'S CHILD Project was doing in Guatemala, and the friend had apparently insisted that Sheen had to meet Patrick.

Patrick parked his bike in front of the Hotel Santa Clara in the center of the city, smoothed down his hair and went inside to the front desk.

"Would you please ring Martin Sheen's room? Tell him Pat Atkinson is here to see him."

Moments later, the famous actor met him in the courtyard of the hotel, hand outstretched. "Patrick? Martin Sheen. I've certainly heard a great deal about you," he said. "I know about the work you're doing with the poor down here and it's an honor to meet you."

Patrick didn't let on that he didn't recognize Martin, but it didn't take the actor long to figure it out for himself. At Patrick's insistence, he rattled off a long list of movies in which he had starred. Patrick had seen part of just one, "Apocalypse Now," and he told Martin that as a missionary he had always identified with the character who, at the beginning of the film, is lying in bed, staring at the ceiling, narrating that he feels tired and burned out, but also recognizing that he can't go home yet.

"That was my character," Martin said, softly. "That was me. I mean that really WAS me back then." At first Patrick felt a little sheepish about not recognizing who Martin was, but quickly realized that Martin did not care. Later, he would tell friends that Sheen was the most humble, approachable, spiritual and down-to-earth man he had ever met. Patrick felt immediately at home with him, as if they had known each other for years.

That morning, as they ate their breakfast they were joined

by the rest of Martin's traveling group. With him were Jesuit writer Fr. John Dear and Fr. Bill O'Donnell, a priest from California who was active in the human rights and national disarmament movements.

When Patrick asked him what he wanted to see, Martin simply said, "Show us your people. Show us who you are."

Patrick said that he would like to take the group to visit Guatemala City's Zona 3 garbage dump, one of the world's worst slums—where an estimated 7,000 people actually lived on top of, beside, and under huge mountains of trash, making whatever living they could from anything of value that they could pick from the piles of refuse.

"But it's too dangerous there," Patrick added with regret.

"If there are people living there, then we should go there, too," Martin said. "Lead the way." They set off in Martin's rental car for the 45-minute trip to the Zona 3 dump.

The smell hit them long before they could actually see the dump. The stench of burning trash wafted out over the neighborhoods surrounding the dump, leaving a smoky haze on a day when there was no breeze. Bad as the smell was, what caused most people to recoil at the first sight of the dump were the people who live there—many of them children, scurrying across the moldering garbage like ants on an anthill. They were so dirty that it was sometimes hard to see where their skin ended and their clothing began. Some wore cloth wrapping for shoes. Others were clearly drunk or drugged out—on heroin or crack if they could afford it, on shoe glue if they could not. A few young girls and women were pregnant, and many had babies clinging to their skirts, the whites of their eyes gleaming from their soot-blackened faces.

At first, it was difficult to tell that there were houses there. Like camouflage, the shacks of cardboard and tin blended almost perfectly with their surroundings, looking like just another pile of debris. But if you watched long enough, you could see that entire families lived there, moving in and out of the shelters. It was where they worked and played, picking through the trash, looking for scraps of metal, pieces of cloth and rotting food.

Martin saw all of this, but he did not hesitate. He waded right into the trash piles, stopping to talk with the people he found there. When he was invited into filthy shacks, he entered, taking a seat on an upended box or broken chair for a brief conversation with the occupants. Knowing that he could not flash money in a place like this and afraid that he might insult his hosts by offering it, he instead pulled out a Polaroid camera and snapped pictures of every person he met, offering the photos as a gift to those with whom he talked. He was quick to smile, and he brought smiles to the faces of the people around him as well. When he left three hours later, he was already discussing with Patrick ways that he could help.

The next day, Patrick agreed to take Martin and his group to the town of Escuintla to visit a priest who was leading a farmer's movement along the coastlands of Guatemala. It was a dangerous trip because the man's actions were not popular with the government or the rich landowners who lived there. Three days earlier, somebody had shot into the priest's house.

"The bullets are still there, embedded in the concrete blocks of his house," Patrick said. "Do you still want to go?"

Martin explained to Patrick why the visit was important, and why he was willing to take the risk.

"I want to offer my support," he said. "It sometime raises the visibility of the people I visit. That way, they know they're not alone, and the people who might hurt them know that their deeds won't go unnoticed. Also, if it's a dangerous business, it's probably also a lonely business," Martin said.

They set out for Escuintla in two cars—the rental car that Martin was driving and Patrick's recently repaired pig truck. There were six of them in the group altogether. Martin, Patrick, and the priests were joined by two other human rights activists. The visit was brief and without incident. Martin offered a donation and encouraging words, as did the others in the group. He exchanged addresses with the farmer's movement leader, took pictures of the bullet holes in the man's front door, and with a wave, left to begin the long drive home.

The plan was to drive directly to Guatemala City, and from there, to drive over the mountain and into Antigua. But as the two cars made their way up the steep mountain grade that took them from Escuintla into the capital city, it began raining hard and traffic slowed. The windshield wipers on Patrick's pig truck didn't work, nor did the defroster. Patrick rolled down the front window and drove the next several miles with his head sticking out of the driver's side.

Several minutes later, Patrick noticed a huge plume of black smoke rolling into the sky farther up the mountainside in front of them.

"Wow, that's really cool. Martin's going to see a volcanic explosion right by the side of the road," he thought to himself. He pulled over and ran back to tell Martin and the others that he thought they were about to see Pacaya Volcano erupting. But then people driving in front of Patrick suddenly started turning their cars around, and others who were on foot came running down the hill.

"What's going on?" Patrick called to one man as he hurried by.

"Guerillas are burning cars!" the man shouted, hurrying away.

Patrick stepped back to the rental car to tell Martin and the priests what he had heard, when somebody else in another retreating vehicle was delayed by downhill traffic just long enough to tell them what he had actually seen with his own eyes.

"No, not guerillas. A passenger bus lost its brakes going down the hill," the man said, "and ran right into a fuel tanker truck. The explosion was huge! That smoke you see is from the fire." That was all Martin needed to hear. He and the others were out of their car and running up the hill with Patrick to see if they could help. The bus was engulfed in a roaring inferno, the passengers unable to escape. Patrick, Martin, and the others stopped in their tracks and could do nothing but watch, horrified. Fr. Dear said a prayer for the dying while Fr. Bill O'Donnell, fearing further explosions, told people to move away from the blazing wreck. Martin and Patrick realized there was little they could do, and Patrick also realized that if they lingered, they could be stuck in mountain traffic for hours. It turned out he was right about that. He later found out that they had just made it out before army trucks arrived, creating a bottleneck that blocked the only route off the mountain. He also heard that 65 people were killed aboard that bus, and that those who were cut off by the army trucks were stuck on the mountain highway for 36 hours, waiting for the accident to be cleaned up.

Because it was getting late and they were upset by what they'd seen, they decided to skip their plans for dinner in Guatemala City, and instead, return to Antigua. But to get past the increasingly heavy gridlock that was forming on the mountainside, they had to take small farming roads through coffee fields and over dried creek beds. It was so bumpy on some of the roads that the windows on the pig truck slipped off their tracks and fell down into the doors. The rain kept up, sometimes pouring, sometimes drizzling into the open windows of the truck, and dripping from the leaky roof.

Not far from Antigua, heading up the mountainside out of

Guatemala City and into the city of Mixco, Patrick's old pig truck simply stopped. The engine went silent and the only sound was the dripping of rainwater onto the pig truck's bare metal rear seat and floor. Patrick coasted to the side of the road and put on the emergency brake. Even that was malfunctioning. The car continued to creep backwards down the hill. To stop it, Martin edged his rental car up behind the pig truck and held it in place on the steep incline. Then, the two of them got out in the drizzling rain to discuss a plan of action. While they stood there, a tow truck happened by and Patrick flagged it down. The driver said he was already on his way to an accident, but he radioed in to his office, and they promised to send another truck within the hour. In the meantime, there was nothing for Patrick to do but wait. He told the others to return to their hotel, but Martin refused to leave.

"We came together, we'll go back together," he said. "Friends don't abandon friends."

He wouldn't even get back in the rental car because there wasn't room for Patrick there. The two of them stood there in the pouring rain on the side of a Guatemalan road, waiting for the tow truck and talking about life. It was a surreal moment, and one that Patrick would never forget.

By the time they arrived back at the hotel and had changed into dry clothes, the restaurant where they planned to eat was filling up. Hungry as they all were, Fr. O'Donnell and Fr. Dear announced that they thought it was a fine time to pray. So, in a corner of the restaurant in front of a Saturday night crowd, the priests put two tables together and celebrated Mass.

During the Sign of Peace, Sheen reached over and handed Patrick $500 in cash.

"Here," he said, "this is to get your car fixed." For Patrick it may as well have been $20,000. Five hundred dollars was an unbelievable gift, and more money than he had seen in one place in several months. He was momentarily speechless, but finally managed to say thank you as he placed the bills in his shirt pocket.

With that evening's Mass barely over, and as they were all getting ready to sit down to dinner in the restaurant, Patrick felt a hand reach over his shoulder into his shirt pocket, and grab the money out. He spun around and saw that it was Martin who had taken his $500 back. Patrick resigned himself to thinking that Martin had regretted making such a large, spontaneous donation.

"I'm sorry," Martin said, "but I shouldn't have given this to you."

"I understand," Patrick replied. "It is a lot of money."

"No, that's not what I mean. What I should have done was offer to buy you a new car. I hope you won't take this as an insult," he continued, "because I know you've worked hard to get this program together, and you have a sense of ownership of it. But you carry valuable cargo in that old truck every day. What if it had been loaded down with kids today when the brakes failed? Or what if something had happened to you while you were driving it? Then where would those kids be? That truck is not safe."

Far from insulted, Patrick said, "Actually, this project isn't mine. It belongs to God. As for the kids and me, absolutely, we would love a new car."

"OK, here's what I want you to do. You tell me what kind of car you want and I'll get it for you. Of course a Toyota would be best," Martin added with a smile. At the time, he was the voice for Toyota. "But it doesn't matter. Just let me know what you want and let me take care of the rest."

Nothing more was said that night, but Patrick kept up his communication with Martin. He did a little research and in a letter, suggested three alternatives: a used car, a new mid-sized car and a 15-passenger Toyota diesel van. Three weeks later, he received a check in the mail for the full price of the brand new 15-passenger Toyota diesel van, given in the name of Martin's wife, Janet.

The political situation in Guatemala that drew activists like Martin Sheen had been going on for generations. It started as a fight to keep land ownership in the hands of a few very wealthy families, while most of the population lived a hand-to-mouth existence. Property owners ran the government, made deals with other nations and directed the military, and the ruling families and individuals fought bitterly to keep this situation as it had been for generations. But government leaders were losing ground. Guatemala's civil war had been raging for 35 years. During those years, 200,000 people had been murdered or simply "disappeared." People who denounced these murders had also "disappeared."

Shortly after Sheen left, Patrick nearly became a "missing" statistic himself because of a mass grave he had discovered years earlier, on property he had purchased for the construction of yet another school.

Patrick first made the discovery in 1989 when he decided to buy land adjacent to the orphanage that he directed. The two pieces of property were separated by an adobe wall and a chicken coop. Patrick ordered them both torn down so that the two properties could become one. But as workers were digging up the floor of the chicken coop, they began unearthing human remains. When they unearthed a skull with an obvious bullet hole, Patrick ordered the digging stopped. He recognized it for what it was—a clandestine cemetery, the shallow graves of murder victims. It was certainly not the first one found in Guatemala, but it was still disturbing. Patrick called the U.S. Embassy and the Archbishop's Human Rights Office. He then called the National Police and also informed the local judge. After he contacted the authorities, plain-clothes policemen came and took away the few bones that had already been unearthed, and that seemed to be the end of it.

When Patrick and his workers uncovered more bones that same weekend, though, Patrick ordered them hidden. By now he had guessed that the authorities were planning a cover-up of what was apparently a very large mass grave. Instinct told him they would not appreciate it if he continued to talk about what he had found. On Sunday, when the orphanage staff and children were at church, he and another volunteer took photographs of each bone, taking care to point out the bullet holes that perforated several of the skulls. After that he ordered the bones reburied where they had been found, and he planted a tree there to mark the spot, just in case somebody should ever ask about them, but nobody did.

Eight years later, two years after Patrick had returned to Guatemala to start The GOD'S CHILD Project, the times and the political environment in Guatemala had changed. Somebody remembered that mass grave, and told the story to the press. As the story circulated, demands were made for a full-scale investigation about who was buried there and why. The courts became involved, and suddenly so did many of the human rights groups that had earlier expressed disinterest in this mass burial ground. Because Patrick was the only original witness with any knowledge of where the bones might be, a judge asked him to help the authorities locate them. The landowner, concerned about property values, was unhappy about all of the publicity, but in the end, he had no choice but to cooperate. The date for the excavations was set, and Patrick agreed to appear on that date and point to exactly where more bones could be found. He noted the date on his calendar, but then didn't give it another thought. He was too caught up in the day-to-day details of running what really amounted to a huge family.

Everything was a learning experience, every outing a chance to teach. As every parent knows, a trip to the grocery store always took twice as long when the kids were with him, and it tended to cost twice as much, too. On the other hand, how else would they learn to bargain hunt and comparison shop? They needed to have a working knowledge of how much things cost.

One evening as he drove from the shopping center to their home, Patrick was leading an impromptu math lesson using their purchases as examples. The boys were talking and laughing as they tried to come up with silly answers, but the conversation came to an abrupt halt at the sound of a loud thud on the side of the van Martin Sheen had bought for the group. They were all startled into silence for perhaps a second or two before one of them asked, "What was that, Patricio?" No sooner had he asked it than Patrick heard the high-pitched whine of a bullet whizzing past the vehicle. Another bullet hit the window frame by his head.

Patrick first stepped on the brake and then, thinking better of that, stomped on the gas pedal as he yelled, "Somebody's shooting at us, for God's sake." His adrenaline was pumping as he speeded back to Antigua. More mad than scared, he stopped at the project's office in Manchen to let the kids off; and as they were gathering up their things and departing for their foster homes in nearby neighborhoods, he took a moment to examine the vehicle. He was disgusted to see a big dent in the side of the brand new van. And, he could see very clearly where a bullet had struck the window frame. Two inches higher and it would have gone through the side window near his head. Two inches lower, and it would have pierced the door and wounded or killed either him or one of the boys. Now he was truly angry. He climbed back in and drove to the police station to file a report. They didn't seem interested, but they took down the information.

The next day he answered a knock on his door, and was greeted by members of a human rights group investigating war crimes. They had heard about the mass graves and asked Patrick if he knew anything about them. Patrick told them he not only knew about the bones, but that he had photographs of them. They stared at him in disbelief.

"And you're the only one who knows where this cemetery is?" they asked.

"Yes, the judge says I'm the only one who knows where the bodies were actually found. And there are more!"

They asked Patrick if he'd had problems because of what he knew, wondering if he'd received any threats. It was then that he told them about the bullet holes in the brand new van.

As soon as he mentioned it, one of them said, "You should go to your embassy. Tell them what happened. They should provide protection for you until the excavations are finished."

Patrick heeded the advice, but he found that his government's embassy was less than anxious to get involved with the investigation into a possible mass cemetery. He then called North Dakota Congressman Earl Pomeroy in Washington, D.C., and told him what had happened.

Congressman Pomeroy took down all of the information, asked Patrick to fax the photos of the bones to him, and said he would take care of it. The next day, the U.S. Ambassador in Guatemala called Patrick and offered protection, a security detail, and an escort out of the country if Patrick wanted one.

But Patrick didn't. He knew that the bones were those of somebody's missing father, somebody's husband, somebody's son.

Patrick was relieved when the day to identify the bones finally came. The property was crawling with television cameras, police officials and human rights activists. Feeling the pressure, at first he drew a blank on where the bones were. He had to close his eyes and concentrate on the land the way it had been six years earlier. Then, instead of imagining a newly planted tree, he imagined a tree that was six years old and walked right to the spot.

"Dig here," he said, sticking a small red flag into the ground.

Some of the officers got down on their knees and began digging with small hand shovels. Within moments, an agent pulled out a human bone and held it above his head to signal the presiding judge. The event made international news.

Not long after that Patrick left the country for a few weeks to visit the United States and found that the media there were very interested in the cemetery story. Most people living in the American Midwest can't really imagine what would drive a person to volunteer for that kind of danger. After hearing about it on the news, Bismarck Sheriff Bob Harvey presented Patrick with a bulletproof vest, and explained certain security steps that Patrick should consider taking. Patrick thanked the sheriff, but said he couldn't imagine wearing it very often.

"Listen to your gut," Sheriff Harvey said. "If you get the feeling that you should wear it, don't hesitate to put it on." Patrick thanked him and agreed to think about it.

When friends suggested he might want to take a little time off, he repeated his standard reply. "If the good run from the bad," he said, "the bad win."

CHAPTER FOURTEEN

Letter to a friend

June, 1992

Dear Lee,

You asked me how things are going in the project. The answer, honestly, is that things are going a little too well. What I mean by that is, we have more children to house, feed and educate every month, and "no" doesn't seem to be a viable part of my vocabulary. Every month I swear I will take in no more kids, and when I say it I really mean it. I know Christ wasn't kidding when he said the poor would be always with us and I know I can't save every poor kid on the streets of Antigua.

But then a young mother comes in with a bedraggled child in tow, and I just can't bring myself to turn her away. I start doing the mental arithmetic. "OK," I'll say to myself, "the cost of keeping her in school next month equals the price of a pizza and a couple of movies. So if this month I eat more ketchup noodles..." And then I find myself saying, "Okay, I'll take her." The thing is, this just has to stop somewhere.

Patrick has always worked around children, so he is not concerned when the judge in Carlitos' case insists that if the little boy is to leave the country, Patrick himself must accompany him. He spends the next couple of days befriending Carlitos so that the child won't be frightened to travel with him. After a couple of days the two are getting along like old buddies. He arranges with Luis to bring Carlitos to The Dreamer Center and they hang out together, although I can see that Patrick is at a loss when, every 20 minutes or so, Carlitos bends over, clutches his belly and wails. All he can really do is hold him until he's quiet, and then wipe his tears. Sometimes Carlitos soils himself, too, and he has to be cleaned up and changed. It is exhausting, and Patrick admits he's not used to it, but it's certainly not the first time he's sat up nights with sick kids.

I ask Patrick whether he ever regrets his decision to stay in Guatemala rather than start a family of his own and he smiles.

"I have a family," he says. "More kids call me Papito than any other father I know." And I realize it's true. He has raised hundreds of kids and founded programs that have raised 18,000 more. When he walks across the yard of The Dreamer Center he is swarmed by children who stop him for a hug. I have seen it a dozen times now. He never turns them away. It can take 10 minutes to stroll the few hundred yards across the school courtyard some mornings, because he stops every few feet to chat with another child. He has lost children that he has loved— to disease, violence and accidents. But he has raised many, too. These days he presides at many weddings and christenings as the children grow up and go on to successful adulthood. To some he has been a foster father, to others a legal guardian.

His legally adopted son, Neto, doesn't live with him full time anymore. Like his father, Neto moves back and forth between their home in Antigua, their apartment in Bismarck, and North Dakota State University where he studies art therapy. It is Neto's summer vacation now, and he is in Antigua volunteering in The Dreamer Center school. Today he is helping out in the outdoor kitchen. He plays with the children as they eat their lunches of donated bread, beans and milk. Everywhere he goes, he gives hugs and leaves children laughing.

Patrick says Carlitos' winning smile reminds him very much of the little boy that his son Neto once was, and he says he will move heaven and earth to try to give them both the futures they deserve. Futures that at one time may have seemed impossible.

"The first time I saw Neto," he says, "I thought he was maybe 5 or 6. Turns out he was 10, but so malnourished that he just hadn't grown. He lived most of his life on the streets," he remembers. "If we hadn't found each other when we did, I doubt he'd be alive today."

Manchen
ANTIGUA, GUATEMALA
1992

The new house and office located at the top of the dusty footpath in the Manchen neighborhood of Antigua was at first a quiet little place. Even though there were already 70 children enrolled in the new project when Patrick and Lorenzo first moved from the farm in June1992, Patrick had found foster families for most of them, and at last these boys and girls were off the streets and in school.

In the new house, Lorenzo made a bedroom for himself out of a small pantry that measured 4-feet wide by 7-feet long, while Patrick used scrap lumber that the two had found along the roadside to build a divider down the middle of the one large room in the back of the house. Patrick slept on the far side of the divider while he and Lorenzo did their work on the other side. Both men used plywood supported by concrete block as beds, and more scrap wood and blocks for shelving and desks. They answered the phone, talked with authorities looking for placement for children found on the streets, they visited with young mothers unable to care for their children, arranged for medical treatment, and prepared food for all who showed up.

And they did show up, at all hours of the day and night. It had not taken long for word to spread that free food was available every day at the project site, which most of the area's street children came to know simply as the house at the top of the hill in Manchen.

Good, safe food is always hard for any street kid to come by, and particularly for the young children who seemed to rule the streets of Jocotenango and parts of Antigua. Most of these boys and girls made what pocket money they could by hustling tourists or store owners, or by offering to watch cars parked outside of the area's many cantinas, where liquor and prostitutes could be had inexpensively.

But there were a lot of homeless and unsupervised youngsters on the streets of Antigua and not nearly enough cars to watch. That meant that hungry street kids were always hanging around the doorway of the Manchen office, peering in at the children who were already inside, clustered around the television set munching on sandwiches. It wasn't long before the newcomers ventured inside as well, although some were more cautious than others.

Patrick looked up from his paperwork one day to see a small boy dash inside, grab a sandwich and run back out and down the street. Patrick had seen him hanging around before. He was a cute little kid with black, curly hair and a wide, infectious grin. His name was Ernesto, or Neto for short. Patrick had tried more than once to talk to him, but the child always avoided him. Finally, he asked one of the other boys why Neto wouldn't stay.

"His mother told him that you would boil him down and make hand lotion out of him," the boy said.

"Hand lotion?" Patrick asked, wanting to laugh. But it wasn't really funny. He knew that rumors often circulated about the foreigners who came to visit or lived in some of the poorer Guatemalan neighborhoods. He knew that the little boy's mother probably believed it. He had heard other children say that white-skinned people ate children, or that they would lure them in, kill them and then sell their body parts to other people around the world.

"Go talk to him!" Patrick told the other boys. "Tell him that I haven't eaten any kids lately. He's pretty skinny and would probably be too bony anyway. Also be sure that he knows I don't use hand lotion," Patrick laughed, "so he's safe." It was a gradual process, but finally, Neto began to come in and sit with the other boys.

Neto slowly learned to trust Patrick, and he began to view him as a parent who could provide the stability and the home that he so badly needed. His mother was often on the streets, shuttling her children from doorway to doorway, looking for food and a warm place where they could sleep.

Neto had spent several months on his own, living on the streets. Some nights he would sleep in the church ruins that dotted the landscape in and around Antigua; other nights he would sleep behind bushes in the park. He always tried to find a place where he wouldn't be spotted and could sleep in relative safety. He wasn't always successful and some days he looked the worse for wear.

Patrick, who had been keeping a close eye on the boy, finally told Neto and another boy named Jorge Mux to sleep on mats on the floor in the corner of the office in the Manchen house at the top of the hill until something more permanent could be arranged. He just slept better at night, knowing those boys were in off the streets. Finally, Patrick did for them what he had done for so many other street children. He found foster families for them and saw to it that they were enrolled in school. For Jorge, the arrangement worked out well, but for Neto, the fit never seemed quite right. He was miserable in his first home where they treated him as a servant. He ran away, so Patrick found a second home for him. That turned out to be a disaster as well. Somehow, Neto always seemed to end up back on the floor of Patrick's office or in the spare bedroom, and as the months passed, the arrangement started to feel permanent.

In January of 1995, Patrick decided to make it legal. To a friend, he wrote:

Dear Sharon;

Well, you're not going to believe this, but I'm thinking about becoming a dad. I know, I know…I'm already a dad many times over to hundreds, maybe thousands of kids, and in a very special way to a baker's dozen or so…but this time I'm thinking about going one step further.

I've been Neto's foster dad, in my own home, for just under three years now, yet I feel like I've known him forever. His birth father died several years ago, and his mother isn't able to care for her four children, so at one time or another they have all lived with me. They are great kids and children that any parent would be proud to call their own.

But Neto is different. Where the others have worked out fine with foster families I've arranged for them, he hasn't. He is slightly older than the others, more street-wise, extroverted, loving, scared and alone. He is back with me now, having challenged his foster family to points beyond what they could handle. To be honest, I was secretly glad to go to their home, pick him up, and bring him home.

Over the years I've learned that where some children are born from their parents' bodies, others are born in their parents' hearts. This is where I think Neto was born into my life.

I don't know if I've ever before been so scared at making a decision. Will he see me as being his father, his guide, and his friend, or will I always be a step-in for his birth father who died when this boy was so young and fragile?

I think that at times like this, it's best to forget about the facts and the fears and listen to the heart. So…what does my heart say? The heart says that Neto was sent to me as a gift from God, to make my life fuller and more complete, to bring depth to my days and fear to the nights when he's out with friends and doesn't come home on time.

The heart also says that I have been asked to be a gift to Neto from God above, to give him direction, stability, encouragement, and the means to make his dreams come true. He might come out of adolescence thinking I'm the worst S.O.B. in the whole wide world, but if he makes it out in one piece, as a good kid with laughter on his face, love in his soul, and at least some direction for his future, then he can think of me what he wants. I'll have done the job that God is asking me to do…to be a parent.

Neto has been good for Patrick. He says being a father gives him the feeling that something of himself will continue, even though they are not related by blood. Raising him hasn't been easy, he says. They have had more than their share of father/son battles, particularly during the teen years, but Neto has also been there for Patrick through good times and bad, helping him with his work, sometimes reaching out to children who won't listen to anyone else. Of all the blessings Patrick thanks God for, he puts Neto right at the top.

CHAPTER FIFTEEN

Monthly Newsletter, December 1998

Snapshots from Lives Changed Overnight

I still remember when the rains began. It was Friday, about three weeks ago, about 6:00 p.m. The skies were much too dark for the early hour. The radio was telling us Hurricane Mitch was about to hit Central America.

By now, you've heard of the devastation of biblical proportions that Mitch caused as it swept through Honduras, Nicaragua, and Guatemala. At The GOD'S CHILD Project in Guatemala, the roads that surround our programs became raging rivers full of logs and rocks and small, broken pieces of people's homes and lives.

Patrick and his assistants, Richard Schmaltz and Javier Alvarado, drive through Carlitos' neighborhood in Altotenango and as they park the car they look around. The street where the family lives is like many that we have seen. The people are very poor. It is difficult to keep anything clean. The main feature is dirt. But bit by bit, The GOD'S CHILD Project volunteers are bringing in new concrete houses. The face of the neighborhood is changing. Patrick would like to see this change extend to Carlitos' family.

"After what we're putting the kid through, I suppose we should build his family a house. Get him off the dirt floor at least," Patrick says.

"He's not on the list to be next," Richard comments, but he agrees, there's little point to saving Carlitos' life only to have him die of an avoidable fever caused by squalor. Richard says he'll assign a service team as soon as he returns to the office.

The GOD'S CHILD Project has always attracted volunteers. These days, most come for a quick mission experience. They pay their own way to Guatemala, spend some time at The Dreamer Center and then journey out to a work site where they labor alongside a local family, building a new home. They are modest houses—most aren't much bigger than an American king-sized bed, but they represent a vast improvement for the families lucky enough to receive them.

Most service teams visit for a week to ten days, and in that time, each group builds one house. It's very hard work. The concrete blocks must be hand carried, sometimes up steep paths where trucks can't go. The volunteers mix and pour the concrete, dig the foundation, build the walls, put on a roof and even build simple wooden bunk beds so that the families can sleep up off the floor. They also put in showers and toilets when they can. Although the plumbing is crude, it's a real step up from the trenches that serve as latrines in most Guatemalan slums.

The service teams require a lot of supervising; and, because they frequently are made up of teenagers and young adults, extra care must be taken to keep everyone safe and healthy. The teams can sometimes seem to be more trouble than they are worth, but Patrick sees their involvement as part of his ministry.

"They frequently don't even pay their way entirely," he says. "If somebody breaks a tool or causes a problem it actually costs us money, and it certainly costs us in man hours. We aren't doing it to get the free labor. We're doing it for the service teams themselves. If they spend a week here, working to improve the lives of one Guatemalan family, then they are forever changed by it themselves. This kind of work brings people closer to Christ. That's why we do it."

The house that volunteers intend to build for Carlitos will be in a new neighborhood. Already, as Patrick makes travel arrangements, plans are in the works for its completion. Like the home of his cousin, Luis, many of the homes in Carlitos' neighborhood are flimsy, built of scraps and odds and ends, but they are relatively new, constructed after 1996, the year that Hurricane Mitch swept entire neighborhoods away. Patrick tells me he thinks of the hurricane as a kind of turning point for him. Once it was over, he says, he began to really believe that what he was building in Guatemala would be permanent.

ANTIGUA, GUATEMALA
1996

When Patrick made his decision in 1991 to return to

Guatemala he never dreamed that his short stay would extend years into the future. He was too busy making ends meet to even think about what was ahead. But slowly, his fledgling project took on the appearance of permanence. Taxed to the limit, he hired more staff to help handle the steadily growing list of children. Volunteers from all over the world came to help him manage the children, and also to help build a brand new headquarters. This time, though, he felt that God was calling him to build something larger, something that would be a permanent base for the project's growing efforts.

His plan called for administrative offices, but he also wanted an oasis for the poor who lived in the surrounding communities. After he chose the piece of land near San Felipe, he began to dream up building designs, which he would scribble onto napkins or paper scraps, whatever came to hand when inspiration struck. At the heart of his ideas was his wish to create a place where people could actually feel God's presence—a peaceful place to counteract the violence, abandonment, abuse, and alcoholism that ran rampant in the area—a place that would help feed children's spirits, as well as their bellies. He took his scribbled design ideas to volunteer contractors who visited Guatemala from the United States and Europe. They began to put his plan into action.

The families of the children who were enrolled in the project did much of the actual labor. Together they cleared the ground, dug the ditches, mixed the concrete using only hoes and garden hoses, and began to raise the buildings. Construction went slowly, as money and manpower became available, but it was steady. Small, adjoining parcels of land were purchased with cash or on credit as they came up for sale.

By 1996, the first set of simple buildings was complete. These were side-by-side two-room classrooms. One of the classrooms was quickly converted into a functional field clinic, and another was put to use as a combination office and storage room until something more permanent could be built. Classes were run out of the other two rooms. The children were fed in a nearby tin-roofed pavilion.

When orphans entered the program, Patrick found foster homes for them and paid these substitute families for the children's upkeep. He also paid for the children's school expenses, bought their uniforms, saw to their medical needs and fed them whenever they stayed late in the project's office doing homework or just talking among themselves.

The Dreamer Center couldn't accommodate all of the children who needed schooling.

So, Patrick enrolled them in neighborhood schools. Not every child was a scholar, though, and it was sometimes hard to make the children understand why education was vital to their futures. Frequently, they stopped going to classes because their parents or foster parents needed them to work in order to earn enough to buy food for the entire family. Tired of paying tuition for children who would drop out after a few weeks, Patrick finally developed a program whereby the families of children who were accepted into the program not only received scholarship money to cover the child's tuition, but they also received a stipend to pay for basic living needs. Although Patrick never cut off the basic living stipend, the children were required to maintain a passing grade in order to receive a tuition scholarship. Those children who did even better than passing, those who maintained higher-than-average grades, received a bonus—money the family could spend any way it wished. It was an incentive program that gave the entire family a stake in the child's education. So long as they stayed in school and received good grades, they were able to bring in more money than any child could earn at a menial job on the streets or in the coffee fields. Patrick called his new method the Bismarck Educational System, or BESY, and it worked so well that within a short time it began to attract international attention.

The plan was to build a school at The Dreamer Center, grade-by-grade, classroom by classroom, so that the children who started in first grade could continue on as they added a grade a year. But much of that progress came to a halt with the arrival of Hurricane Mitch. It caught many in Guatemala by surprise.

Among them, was Sandrita Manchu . She had heard the warnings on the radio, but paid little attention. She was too busy with the day's washing, and with preparing breakfast for her two children who had awakened her at 6 a.m., complaining about their empty bellies. She had tried to ignore them, but since all three of them shared the same bed, it wasn't easy. She could hear their stomachs rumbling. With a sigh, she pushed herself up out of bed and shuffled her feet into dirty, plastic sandals. She took just a moment to splash water on her face from the cold-water faucet in the yard, and twisted her hair into a knot at the back of her head. Then she shooed the kids out of her way while she warmed up last night's beans and rice.

"Go! I'll call you in a few minutes," she said, giving her older son a light swat on the fanny to move him along. The boys ran out into the yard to chase a puppy, their stomachs momentarily forgotten.

Now, Sandrita sighed as she looked at the pile of laundry by the communal sink. She had no husband, and was only 17. She became pregnant with four-year-old Luis when she was only 12, and the boy's father had been little more than a child himself. She had not heard from him in a long time. She had dropped out of school when she started to show and had not been back since. She stayed home with her mother and her aunts and sisters. It was a household of women—not unusual in Guatemala, where the men often left one day to go into the city to find work, and then did not come back. If they did come back, it was once or twice a year. Just long enough to impregnate their women, and then leave again for the city. The men in Sandrita's family were not inclined to live up to their responsibilities, so the women took in washing to earn money to buy food.

Sandrita turned the faucet handle that started the flow of cold water. Already, her hands were turning red in the chilly morning air, but she did not notice. She flattened a shirt out on the washboard, took a bar of soap down from the ledge above and began scrubbing, pausing to shove loose locks of hair out of her face with her wrist. The children had finished eating and were squabbling over a stick, but she ignored them, lost in her own thoughts.

This afternoon she had an appointment at The GOD'S CHILD Project Dreamer Center, where she planned to enroll her second child in school. Now that he was weaned, she looked forward to the free time that she would have if he were gone for part of the day. He was getting too big to carry on her back all day. He squirmed too much, but when she put him down he tended to run off and then she had to go looking for him. They would also feed him at the center, which would be a big help to her. Of course, she knew she would have to spend that free time working, but it would be nice to have some money of her own instead of always depending on her mother and her aunts. She looked down again at her chapped hands and thought it would also be good to get away from this concrete sink, and these stinking clothes. Just yesterday she had met a rich American in the market who said he was looking for maids for the new house he was building in Jocotenango.   He had smiled at her in a familiar way, and had offered her a ride home in his red Toyota. She thought he would hire her.   She tried not to think much beyond that.

She was just finishing her first pile of laundry and was about to start on a second when the first raindrops fell on the sheet-plastic roof that covered the wash area.   It didn't seem to be a bad storm at first, just persistent, with steady rain.   But it was a persistence that would prove deadly.   It rained, and it rained, and it rained some more.

The people who lived in Sandrita's neighborhood, on a hillside overlooking Antigua, had homes that were constructed mainly of tin and concrete blocks, filled in here and there by corrugated cardboard and scraps of whatever else the family could find.   It was fenced in by dried cornstalks, lashed together with twine.   The floors and walkways were hard-packed dirt, and inside the houses it was cramped and dark.   The families slept three and four to a bed—sometimes more.   The Manchu family had electricity, which they "rented" from a neighbor.   That neighbor was the one with electrical hook-up, and Sandrita's mother had talked him into allowing her access to a single outlet, to which she attached an extension cord, and for which she paid a monthly fee.   The extension cord ran across both yards and disappeared up under the eaves of the Manchu's cardboard house.   At least the radio was staying dry.

Most of the family's worldly goods were stored around the

yard outside, under large sheets of plastic that Sandrita and her sisters had salvaged from a construction site, but as the days wore on, and the rain did not quit, things inside and out began to get soggy.

Finally Sandrita paid attention. This was no monsoon rain. It was Hurricane Mitch. Day after day, Sandrita and her mother and aunts listened to the radio announcer talk about the rising water. Rivers were starting to overflow their banks. Topsoil ran downhill, filling streams and plugging underground septic systems. The water tables were rising, which meant that most privies also overflowed and became streams of filth that ran right through people's houses on their way downhill. Trash from garbage pits was washed into the streets of Antigua and other Guatemalan cities. The waste-filled mud became so thick that walking was nearly impossible. Those who tried found themselves knee deep in a sucking quagmire.

People who could, left the mountainsides and sought shelter on more solid ground, but not the Manchus. They had no place to go. They huddled under wet blankets and sheets of plastic, drinking dirty water and eating moldy food. Before long the children had diarrhea, fevers, and croupy coughs, and there was nothing that Sandrita could do to help them.

Still, the rain kept falling. The clay tiles on the roofs of more permanent buildings became saturated with water, and started to leak. The ground grew so soft and spongy that people could sink a stick 18 inches into what days before had been hard-packed earth. Finally, the houses along the hillsides—the homes of both rich and poor alike—began to slide downhill.

Sandrita heard the mountainside collapsing before she felt or saw it. It was like the sound of distant thunder at first, but she had little time to wonder at it before the earth beneath her seemed to tip and slide, taking her and her boys and her mother and aunts along with it. She grabbed for her children's hands, but they were soon wrenched from her grasp and were sliding away from her, down into the mud, while all of their belongings tumbled down with them and then on top of them. When Sandrita finally came to rest at the bottom of the ravine she realized that one of her children had landed on top of her. He was so caked with slimy mud that she couldn't tell which one it was at first. She scraped debris from his nose and mouth and covered him with her body as the mountainside continued to rain down on them for several more minutes. When the earth finally stopped moving it seemed very quiet at first, and yet it was not, because she could still hear the steady beat of the rain. But she could not hear her children. The one under her was breathing, but limp, his eyes closed. The other, she could not see at all. She began calling for him frantically, but he did not answer. Her mother rose up out of the mud some distance off, dazed, but not seriously hurt, and Sandrita could see her aunts moving also. They had not fallen from a great distance, but tons of topsoil now rested at the bottom of the ravine, burying everything, including little Luis. Sandrita wrapped her younger child up in a sarape and slung him on her back, then started digging. Friends and neighbors who had survived the slide down the hill joined in the search, but it would be two days before they found the little boy's body, buried under a thick layer of mud and debris.

It seemed as if the entire mountainside washed down that day. The people living in the San Felipe slums didn't have much to begin with. When the water and mud poured down, it carried away people's entire lives—their cooking utensils, blankets, clothes and livestock. There was no place to go to get out of the rain, no dry place to sleep, no food to eat. People began streaming, dripping and muddy, into The Dreamer Center.

Patrick had been dealing with his own storm problems. He had been busy trying to save the new clinic building. Still under construction, the foundation walls were in danger of collapsing, so great was the pressure of the water-saturated mud that pressed against the side of the unsupported structure. He was talking with engineers about how to shore things up when he caught sight of the crowd at the gate and realized what was happening. He forgot the wall and instead, invited people into the community room. It was about the only dry space he could find. He called his staff and volunteers together and one by one, sent them off to help each family save what it could. Later, when he learned that many of the families had no place to live, he ordered all construction stopped and instead, offered refuge to flood victims in whatever space was available in The Dreamer Center compound. Half-built classrooms became temporary shelters for dozens.

Hour after hour, staff members and volunteers dug in the dirt, looked for lost children, gathered blankets, prepared soup, handed out medicine, and filled out paperwork seeking assistance for those who had lost everything. Each night several dozen homeless people slept in the safety of the unfinished Dreamer Center, using half-built walls for shelter and donated blankets and firewood for warmth. The storm stalled over Central America for days, killing 11,000 people, and leaving more than two million homeless. In Guatemala itself, the official death toll was only 197, but in reality, it went much higher in the days and weeks that followed, as people died of disease and despair.

Eighty thousand Guatemalans were washed out of their homes during that single storm. Because Hurricane Mitch hit during harvest time, the bananas, coffee, corn, and tobacco were destroyed and left to rot in the fields. Farm workers not only lost their houses, thousands of them also lost their jobs, and many of them were left homeless, forced to sleep in the doorways of churches or downtown shops and forage for food for themselves and their families. They also heard that help was available at The Dreamer Center, and long lines formed outside, the people looking for bread, clothes, and assistance.

Many other international programs closed down after Hurricane Mitch, saying that they needed the time to themselves to clean up. But at The Dreamer Center, business continued, although altered to fit the needs of the refugees. The clinic wall did not collapse, but construction was halted for a time, as Patrick and the other volunteers focused their efforts on helping people to reestablish their lives.

When construction began again, Patrick decided to shift the emphasis of the work that volunteers would do. He switched to the service team approach and welcomed people of all ages from all over the world to come and help rebuild neighborhoods destroyed by Hurricane Mitch. Slowly, life returned to normal, one house at a time. And soon, it would be Carlitos' family's turn.

CHAPTER SIXTEEN

National News Report

Guatemala City – At least six inmates are dead and 15 injured in a bloody prison riot Wednesday near Guatemala City. At least four of the inmates were decapitated during the four hour stand-off with police. Bystanders reported hearing occasional shots or explosions coming from inside the prison.

A police spokesman said that officers fired tear gas into the prison yard to quell the riot and were finally able to retake the facility.

"It's a situation of chaos," said one firefighter, coughing, his eyes streaming from exposure to the tear gas...

"If I had a dime for every thug in Guatemala who has vowed to kill me, I'd sure be able to afford a better car," Patrick says after learning that he's been threatened by El Pato, the man who shot Carlitos. He received the warning from a friend who worked in the Attorney General's office.

"He's likely to get the death penalty, but I guess he wants to take me with him," Patrick adds. He appears to take the warning with a grain of salt, but I wonder how much of that is bravado. On the other hand, Dwayne Walker and I were with him one morning when he visited one of the prisons. He waltzed in like he hadn't a care in the world. Only someone who knows him well would have seen his nervousness. He continually scanned the scene, being careful not to let anybody in the prison yard get too close, and with good reason. Some of these men are in the prison because he testified against them. So while he brings fresh food, medicine, soap and toothpaste, he is also a thorn in the sides of a number of these inmates. This visit ends without incident.

"I may think twice the next time I enter the prison where El Pato is currently residing, though," he tells us as we drive back through Antigua on our way to the Dreamer Center. "No matter how much good will you build up, the truth is that you're taking your life in your hands every time you go through those locked gates." The stories he relates next say something about his character. He is no shrinking violet.

CHIMALTENANGO, GUATEMALA
1993

Patrick really disliked visiting the prisons, and he particularly disliked the prison at Chimaltenango because it was so far from town. He had been there many times before—usually to intervene in some crisis—and he had established a good working relationship with the prison staff. They didn't necessarily always trust one another, because their views on how prisoners should be treated were so vastly different, but they did understand each other. Patrick was one of the few foreigners that the prison staff allowed to enter. On his frequent visits, he always brought enough blankets, food, soap, or toothpaste for both the prisoners and the guards, so his arrivals were always moments of excitement. In return for his discretion and sensitivity in dealing with the problems confided to him by both the prisoners and the guards, he was frequently asked to stop and visit with prisoners who were in trouble.

On this night, as Patrick drove the familiar road, he thought about the first time he had intervened to get kids out of prison. He was dead tired that night, because he had spent the previous night in a hospital ward, sitting beside a sick child's bed trying to write letters to benefactors. The room had been cold and his neck was stiff from nodding off while sitting up in the straight-backed chair. As soon as it appeared that the child was out of danger, Patrick left the hospital in the early hours of the morning to visit the boy's frightened mother. After that his top priority was to get some rest, so he chased away several of the kids who had accompanied him to church and he returned home, nearly falling over with fatigue. He had just sat down on the side of his bed to remove his shoes when his phone rang. It was a friend of a friend, telling him that two of the project's boys had been arrested and were being held in the Chimaltenango National Prison.

"Why would they take kids to a men's prison?" he asked.

"Nobody asked their ages. They made the cops mad, and

neither of them was carrying any papers with them to show their real ages. A stupid combination, I guess, walking without documents and showing a little bit too much attitude," the friend answered.

"What did they do?" Patrick asked.

"They say they were busted for theft of property," the friend responded. "Not sure what that means, but they don't have anyone to work on getting them out of there."

Patrick looked at the clock hanging on his bedroom wall and sighed. He was so tired he wasn't even sure that he would be able to safely drive the rough rural roads to the prison, much less muster the energy to be effective when he got there. He lay down, sighed again, and stared at the ceiling. It was cracking, he noticed, and water was surely going to leak in when the rains started in May. Every muscle ached, and he wanted more than anything else to close his eyes and sleep. "Just for one minute," he thought.

Feeling himself nodding off, Patrick sat up with a start, heart pounding in his chest. He had almost fallen asleep, and if he did, he knew he wouldn't wake up for several hours, certainly not until late into the night. He knew what he had to do. Standing up, he wasted no time gathering whatever first aid supplies he could find lying around his home, grabbed whatever food he could find to make sandwiches for what he was sure would be a couple of very hungry teenage boys, pulled some of his clothing off the racks for them to use, and headed to his car to begin the rough ride to prison.

In the Chimaltenango National Prison, as in all Guatemalan prisons, the inmates are tossed in together, as if in a vast cage, regardless of their crimes. The door is locked behind them and each prisoner quickly learns that he is there alone, forced to fend for—and defend—himself. Patrick knew what was happening to those boys in there. But even if he worked fast, he also knew that it would be several days before he could get them out. First, he had to round up enough cash to interest an attorney in defending them, and to plead a case for them to be released on bail. Then, there would be the court hearings, and the judges would need several days to render a decision. None of this was soon enough for Patrick. Something had to happen quickly to get these kids the protection they needed.

Arriving at the Chimaltenango National Prison's front gates, Patrick showed his national identity card to get in the front door, and then moved toward the inspection table. He watched while the sandwiches were searched, most of the medicine was confiscated, and the clothing he had brought for the boys was tossed around. Finally the gates were opened just wide enough for him to slip through, and once he was inside, they were just as quickly slammed shut behind him. Being the only foreigner there and carrying food, medicine, and clothing, Patrick immediately felt several dozen sets of menacing eyes fix directly on him.

"OK, God," he thought. "I know we're not supposed to be afraid to walk through the valley of death, but please don't let it be now."

Locked behind the heavy steel prison gates, Patrick could see his two boys sitting in the far corner of the prison yard. They were alone, neither boy quite facing the other prisoners, yet trying to look in all directions at all times. They were thin, tired, and looked as though they had been roughly treated, either by the police or the inmates. "Most likely the inmates," Patrick thought. Knowing how life is behind prison bars, he automatically guessed that both boys had been sexually molested as well. It seemed that nearly every new prisoner was molested—in a way that was almost ritualistic.

One of the boys, José Gutierrez, offered Patrick a faint smile when he looked across the prison courtyard and saw Patrick standing there, looking back at him. The other, Martin Calan, continued to look down, perhaps not knowing Patrick was there, or perhaps feeling a sense of shame that prevented him from looking up into the face of the man who had raised him. Eventually Martin did raise his head and simply stared at Patrick with a bewildered expression. Both boys were clearly exhausted and appeared sick and scared.

Mustering up courage, matched with at least the appearance of bravado, José suddenly stood up and called out across the courtyard. "Hey, Viejo. Here we are." Affecting a cocky gait, José swaggered over to where Patrick stood and reached out his arm to shake hands. Patrick knew better than to give one of his boys a hug on the prison courtyard grounds.

"What happened?" Patrick asked them after they were joined by Martin.

José answered, "We were so stupid. We saw a bicycle sitting up against the wall of a house. We thought it would be fun to take it for a spin. We brought it back, but by then they had already called the police. We tried to run, and that just made it worse," he said.

"Why did they bring you here?" Patrick asked.

"Martin said something that one of the cops didn't like, so first they beat us up, and after that they tossed us in here." Patrick was allowed to give the boys the basic first aid supplies that he had brought. Then he gave them a small amount of cash, along with careful instructions he had learned from the hundreds of prisoners he had visited with and cared for over the years. After he told them how to take better care of themselves, he told them to use the money to buy prison crafts from the inmates.

"You've got to be crazy," Martin said, his eyes flashing angrily. "Do you know how these guys have been treating us? I don't want to give them any money. I want to kill them."

"Listen," Patrick said. "I understand. I really do, but if you just listen to what I'm telling you, you're going to find that life will become easier from here on out.

"I can't get you out of prison today, and I don't know how long it's going to take to do that. I will get you out, but it will take a while. Why didn't you call me earlier?"

"We were ashamed," José answered without delay.

"We thought we could get ourselves out of here," Martin added. "I mean, we did get ourselves in here, didn't we?" Both boys laughed nervously.

"Here's what you need to do," Patrick continued. "Take this money that I'm giving you today and spread the word that I'm a rich gringo who wants to buy a lot of prison crafts. Talk softly and only tell one or two people, so that it sounds like a secret. Be sure to mention that I made you two my purchasing agents for the prison crafts, and that you'll be doing all the purchasing for me. If you tell me to buy from someone, I'll buy. If you tell me not to buy from someone, I won't. But don't tell many people—maybe just one or two. Let the rumor spread. Next week I'll come again and bring as much money as I can, so that people take you seriously. After that, I'll do the best I can.

"You're going to be my purchasing agents, you hear?" Patrick emphasized once again. "People treat you well, we buy from them. People treat you badly, we don't. That's a language that any prisoner anywhere in the world can understand. Now do you understand?" he asked.

Both boys understood what Patrick was doing for them. Both nodded their heads.

"Tell them there's more money where that came from," Patrick said, pressing his money into their hands, "and that I'll buy whatever they can make as long as you, my purchasing agents, tell me what to buy."

"What happens after that?" Martin asked.

"That gives me time to go to the judge and try to get you guys out of here," Patrick answered.

His plan worked. The boys, now carrying folding cash, quickly gained friends who protected them from the other inmates. Those who had been hurting the boys didn't quite apologize, but they suddenly started to talk to José and Martin as if they were equals, not victims.

It took Patrick several weeks to arrange their release, and in that amount of time, he used every cent he had received as Christmas gifts from his family back in the United States, and borrowed money from everybody he knew. During those long weeks, Patrick visited the boys every Thursday and Sunday and always took them lunch—usually fried chicken and a soda. He knew his plan was a good one when, near the end of the boys' stay in prison, several prison guards brought out homemade crafts that they had made themselves, wanting José and Martin to sell them. Finally, it appeared that the boys were going to be safe and protected until their release.

The boys' stay in the prison had another, unintended effect. Long after they were released into Patrick's custody and he had taken them back to Antigua, one of the guards at the prison remembered his name and called him again, this time to tell him about a prisoner who was delirious and apparently dying from a laceration on his foot.

"What can I do to help?" Patrick asked, concerned about the prisoner but confused as to what they wanted him to do about it. He wasn't a doctor, after all.

"I don't know," the guard said, "but please do something. Get him a doctor. The guy's foot looks like it's rotting, and he's noisy too, keeping all of the other prisoners awake. He's making everybody edgy."

So, Patrick got into his car and drove to the prison, walked up to the gates, and asked to see the prisoner. At first the nighttime warden refused, but Patrick convinced him that if the man died, it would be on his watch, which meant investigations, added paperwork, and countless explanations.

"Maybe I can help him," Patrick added, pointing to the first aid kit that he carried in his hand. Reluctantly, the warden unlocked the doors and let him in, then turned him over to the guards who took him to the back of the prison where the sick man lay on a filthy mattress in a dark corner.

"Hey, amigo, how are you feeling?" Patrick asked, bending over the man and trying hard not to inhale his stench. He had the sickly smell of rotting skin about him, in addition to the stale odors of sickness and unwashed flesh. The man did not answer. He lay on his mattress, mumbling and moaning feverishly.

"Where's he hurt?" he asked the guard, who nodded in the direction of the man's foot. It was dim, but even without the flashlight that Patrick brought he could see the problem. The foot had a large gash on the bottom, which had festered and was crawling with maggots that had already worked their way past the surface tissue. Several lines of infection ran up the man's leg, and the skin around the cut was turning black.

"Looks like gangrene," he said to the guard, who nodded. Gangrene was something Patrick had seen quite often during the war years. "He needs to get to a hospital right away, or he isn't going to make it," Patrick continued.

"The warden says no. He says he doesn't have any authorization to let a man out of prison, and the contract doctor doesn't want to come in here at night."

"He needs more than a doctor," Patrick insisted. Drawing on his acting skills, he improvised as he went along, "He needs to get to a hospital. See that infection line there? In about three hours that is going to hit an artery and then it's going to go into the man's heart. Once there it's going into the third and fourth chambers and those are going to pump the infection around his body. He's going to get gangrene everywhere, even in his blood. He needs to be on antibiotics right away, and the kind you get in a pill or squirting out of a needle isn't going to be strong enough. He needs to get an I-V line into him, or he's a dead man by morning."

The prison guard stepped back, angry and frightened at the prospect of being blamed for this man dying. Patrick was also nervous, but for an entirely different reason. He knew that the wound was serious and probably gangrenous, but he had made the rest up in order to stress the urgency of the situation to the prison authorities. He must have been convincing. Thinking Patrick might also be a doctor, the guard decided they had better get the man medical care right away.

"Still," the guard said, "the warden isn't going to want to take a man out without permission."

"Let me try to talk to him," Patrick responded. They walked back to the front of the prison where the warden now sat with his feet on the desk, flipping through a magazine.

"So, what did you find?" he asked with little interest.

"You have a man back there who will die, probably tonight, unless he goes to the hospital right away. His foot is literally rotting off," Patrick replied.

"Well, as I explained to my friend here," said the warden, nodding in the guard's direction, "I have no authorization to take this man out of prison tonight. What if this is an escape plan?"

"Have you seen the guy? He's not going anywhere," Patrick replied. "He can't hobble much less walk or run. He doesn't even know his own name."

"Even so, I can't take the responsibility. It could mean my job."

"Look," Patrick tried again, "do you want this guy's death on your conscience or on your shift? Because that's the direction he's headed." The warden refused to be swayed.

Patrick had an idea.

"I know you don't want to take responsibility for this. How

about if I go over to the shift judge and file a human rights complaint against the prison? The judge will call you in, you explain your situation and that your hands are tied, and he'll issue you an order to take the man to the hospital. You'll have to let him out then, but it won't be your decision or your responsibility."

The warden thought about it for a moment, thought about the dying man and finally nodded in Patrick's direction.

Fortunately, Patrick knew the judge, so it didn't take long to get the court order, mandating that the warden send the man to the hospital—escorted, the judge had added, by four armed guards. Leaving the courthouse, Patrick shook hands with the judge and drove back to the prison where he helped to get the dying man into his car, waited while the prison guards packed overnight bags, and then drove everyone in the project van to the Antigua National Hospital where he was forced to pay for the man's initial care.

That incident opened Patrick up to a flood of requests from prisons throughout the region. Whenever anybody, prisoner or prison authority alike, needed an advocate for a prisoner, he was called. Every time he visited the prisons he brought food or toiletries—sometimes medicines.

At the prison in Antigua, the physical conditions were particularly bad. The inmates were housed in a 500-year-old church ruin, and it was literally crumbling down around them. The first time Patrick saw it there was little running water—

THE DREAM MAKER   223

barely a trickle from the ancient pipes. The toilets were all broken off and had never been repaired, which meant that the prisoners were squatting over broken, jagged, porcelain shards. The electrical system was also poor, and there were stinking piles of trash everywhere. He could see the despair that existed inside the prison. He befriended the warden and over time, earned his trust. He then floated a proposition by him.

"I think I can find somebody to come in here and fix this place up a little, fix the plumbing, bring in electrical, maybe even a TV so that the prisoners have something to do."

"And in return?" the warden asked.

"In return, I'd like you to find a safe place where my volunteers can teach some of these inmates to read."

The warden stared at him in astonishment. "Why?" he asked.

"Because I think an education could be the key to a different kind of life for some of these men. It might help them to get a better job. At the very least, it will give them something to do, and maybe make them feel better about themselves. It might also make your job easier."

"How so?"

"Think about it. Less boredom, less trouble," Patrick answered. The warden did think about it. It made sense. He talked to the prison authorities, and Patrick's plan went into high gear. Patrick and the project's volunteers spent the next three years making major and minor repairs in the prison, and over time, dignity and human respect became more apparent within the 500-year-old ruin. At the same time, a reading program started.

He told a visiting reporter, "It's still not nice by any means, but at least there's some dignity. The men can stay clean—they can watch a little TV, they can study, maybe learn something. I think they appreciate it."

"Why are you doing this?" the reporter asked Patrick. "Most people hate prisoners and couldn't care less what happens to them."

"I'm a really simple man," Patrick responded calmly. "I really am. We do what we do in the prisons simply because Christ asked us to. During the Sermon on the Mount, he told us to feed the hungry, heal the sick, and visit those who are imprisoned. So we do it. It really is that simple."

After a slight pause, Patrick softly added, "Don't forget that these are people too. Many of them are in here because they got drunk and did something stupid, or maybe got into a fight. It doesn't make them bad people."

Not everybody appreciated his efforts, though. Some of the prisoners were there because they'd made bad choices, some got some tough breaks, but others were truly evil, or were mentally disturbed and could be very violent. Some people, Patrick learned, just seemed to be without normal human emotion.

One day Patrick was called to visit a prisoner, and as he walked to the back of the prison, he paid little attention to the men playing soccer in the yard. He had never visited during the day when there wasn't a soccer game in progress. It was just part of the prison atmosphere. The men who spent time in this prison learned to be experts at soccer simply because there was nothing better to do.

He never saw the ball come at him. It smashed into the side of his head, breaking his nose along with his glasses, and shattering one of the bones in his cheek. It sent him flying against a stone wall, and then down onto the ground where he lay unconscious for several seconds.

"Sorry!" he faintly heard someone in the group call out sarcastically, but wracked with pain and bleeding from his eyes, nose and mouth, he was in a fog and couldn't really tell who had said it.

A guard's whistle blew and suddenly the large steel gates burst open. Several guards poured into the courtyard where Patrick lay, as the 150 prisoners instinctively followed their routine and lined up against the wall outside of their three large dormitories.

The guard who led him back to the entrance whispered in his ear, "It's only a guess, but I'd say somebody doesn't appreciate those medicines and supplies you've been bringing into the prison."

"Who?" Patrick asked, holding a handkerchief to his bleeding eyes and nose while wiping at the tears that were streaming down his face.

"Think about it, Patrick. Who stands to gain by you NOT bringing in medicines and supplies?" the guard asked in return.

"Those prisoners who were playing?" Patrick asked, confused at first. But then he understood. Prior to Patrick's becoming involved in visiting and helping the prisoners, a few privileged prisoners had been smuggling in and selling black market supplies and medicines to the few inmates who could afford them. Their mark-up was tremendous, so for months or years they had been making a nice profit. Patrick was now cutting into that. That soccer ball, carefully aimed at the side of his face, had not been an accident.

"They want you to be intimidated. If you think it's too dangerous here, they figure you won't be back."

But he was back the very next week, his nose and glasses taped up, a huge bruise across the side of his face. The only difference was that from then on he never again felt comfortable when he was inside the prison walls. He never forgot that some of these men were violent—and that some were very unstable. He didn't want to go in, because now he was afraid. Still he kept going in and taking in the medicines, foods, and blankets. He kept on fixing the old rusted pipes when they burst. But now it was a little more difficult to see Christ's face.

"Christ sometimes hides a little deeper," Patrick told the

volunteers, "so sometimes we need to look a little harder to find Him. He's always there, though, so be sure to say 'hi.'"

His international reputation as an advocate for prisoner's rights grew. In a letter to his board of directors, Patrick wrote:

> *"I have been asked to be on the negotiating team that is trying to quell and prevent the prison riots that seem to be sweeping across Guatemala right now. I can't say that it isn't dangerous. The prisons are powder kegs just waiting to explode. But both sides trust me to bargain in good faith, so unless you object, I plan to help."*

GOD'S CHILD Project board members reacted with concern over what could happen to Patrick inside the national prisons during a time of violent rioting. In the end, though, they agreed that if Patrick felt prison work was part of the project's mission to serve the poor, they would not tell him to stop.

Patrick's work in the prisons has been recognized at the highest levels, and he has received national and international human rights awards, recognizing the changes that he and his volunteers have brought to Guatemala's prisons.

In his parting words to the reporter covering his prison work, Patrick said, "The awards are just a different way of saying thank you. Those words, 'thank you,' we now hear prayed each day inside the prison walls. If only we could work together and pray together before people make the mistakes that send them to prison, the work would be so much easier, wouldn't it?"

CHAPTER SEVENTEEN

Letter to The GOD'S CHILD Project Board of Directors

June 1998

Dear Members of the Board of Directors,

Well, it will probably come as no surprise to you, but once again I am going to have to change houses. One of the prisoners that I was working with in the Antigua National Prison was recently released, and he is now coming to my front door six or seven times a day. I've helped him in whatever ways I can, but he is getting more aggressive, insisting we let him come into the house to rest. His eyes are darting... his face has a twitch. Mercedes Ordoñez, the security man who has worked inside of our house for the past three years, says that he sees this man standing down on the corner at the end of the street for several hours each day and night, though we don't know what for...

On the morning that Patrick, his assistant Eric Chittle and Carlitos leave Guatemala for Bismarck, the little boy is having a particularly bad day. His stomach is more upset than usual, probably from nervousness, but it's causing Patrick to pace in the airport in Guatemala City as they wait for their flight to be called. Eric Chittle is coming along because he needs medical attention himself, and also because Patrick wants to make sure that Carlitos has somebody whom he knows with him at all times.

Patrick is accustomed to being responsible for kids, but this time, he knows if something happens to Carlitos, if he fails to return him as promised, he will have to answer to the Guatemalan authorities and also to the little boy's family.

He offers Carlitos some toys to play with, but the boy is in too much pain to really focus on them. He bends down and clutches his belly and Patrick picks him up and carries him into the restroom to change the little boy's now soiled clothes. Outside in the waiting area, Carlitos' screams of pain are clearly audible. Eric pretends not to notice, but all eyes are on Patrick when he leaves the restroom with the child.

"He's still sick," he says to Eric in a voice loud enough for everyone to hear. Fortunately, Carlitos chooses that moment to vomit on himself, and the sideways looks from onlookers who had been suspicious now turned sympathetic. A young mother asks Patrick what is wrong and wonders if she can help. He smiles his thanks, and explains that Carlitos is heading to the United States for medical treatment. The young woman pats Carlitos on the back for a moment and returns to her seat. Finally they board the plane and Carlitos dozes off, but it is a fitful sleep, broken by fits of weeping, vomiting and diarrhea. Two plane changes and many hours later, the exhausted group straggles off the airplane in Bismarck, only to be greeted by reporters with lights and cameras. Even though it is nearly midnight, the story of the orphaned little boy has touched a chord with the community and his sleepy face will be on morning news programs. Tired as he is, Carlitos smiles for the cameras and accepts the gift of a teddy bear from Chuck and Tip Reichert, the Bismarck family waiting to welcome him as a guest into their home.

Early the next morning, Patrick carries the little boy into the hospital where he is greeted by another crowd of reporters. The hospital has arranged a news conference and Carlitos, sick and exhausted, falls asleep on Patrick's shoulder in the middle of the introductions. He wakes a short time later, though, crying and clutching his belly. Patrick wipes the child's tears and says to the reporters, "This has happened every 20 minutes for months now. Can you imagine how exhausted he must be?" From the news conference, Carlitos is carried into an exam room and his treatment begins. Hours pass, and later that day, reporters are again summoned to the hospital for a condition report.

"The first thing we did," says Dr. Cunningham, "was try to make him more comfortable by giving him drugs that would calm his bladder spasms." He explains that the spasms were caused, at least in part, by the catheter that had been in Carlitos' bladder for months. It was adult sized, which meant that it had been irritating the bladder and causing intense discomfort every time he'd had the urge to urinate or move his bowels.

"As soon as we did that," he says, "we saw a remarkable change in the child. He felt better almost immediately."

Before Dr. Cunningham can operate, he explains that the little boy's system must be cleared of parasites, which are common to nearly all poor children in Guatemala. They also want to give him time to regain his strength with good food and uninterrupted sleep.

It is two weeks before the surgery takes place. When Dr. Cunningham does operate, he finds that the little boy's urethra has been shot in two, but fortunately, the other bullets had passed through his body and the wounds healed without leaving lasting damage. First the scar tissue is removed and then Dr. Cunningham sews the severed ends of his urethra back together. The catheter is removed two days later. The first time Carlitos urinates normally, he hollers in excitement. "Come see, come see!" he cries. And it is cause for celebration. It is a giant step on the little boy's road to healing.

By now, Carlitos is also relaxing into his surroundings and in the days that follow, his appetite returns and gradually, he learns how to trust that his play time will not be interrupted by pain. What doesn't go away, though, are his nightmares. Every night he wakes, sometimes many times, screaming, "El Pato! El Pato!" Patrick and Eric sleep in beds nearby, and take turns getting up to comfort him. As Patrick holds him and listens to the details of the little boy's bad dreams, he experiences nightmares of his own.

ANTIGUA, GUATEMALA
1998

A bulletproof vest is hot and heavy and can itch like crazy, particularly the older models. They chafe the skin and don't allow sweat to dry. Patrick hated wearing one. Yet he was told by professionals that he needed to take extra security steps whenever he went outside.

While he was working in his office late one afternoon, the phone rang. It was the warden at "El Infiernito," Guatemala's highest security national prison, built on a hot and humid piece of forgotten land down in the subtropical coastal lands of Escuintla.

"You need someone to watch your back," the man said as soon as Patrick answered the phone.

"Again?" Patrick laughed as he continued sorting through the piles of correspondence on his desk. He thought he had heard it all before. In his human rights and legal advocacy work across the Guatemalan countryside, he and his staff frequently worked to derail the deadly efforts of drug dealers, street gangs and child molesters. As part of that, he frequently testified against them. It was often his testimony that led to a conviction, since the other witnesses in the criminal cases were frequently frightened into not appearing in court, or into "forgetting" the details of the case. The convicted almost always vowed revenge.

Ironically, it was almost always GOD'S CHILD Project volunteers who later provided these very same prisoners with blankets, food and medical care in the nation's prisons. While accepting of, and dependent upon the help that Patrick and his volunteers provided, the convicts didn't forget who helped to put them in prison in the first place. He knew that their bitterness could cost him dearly. The never-ending pain from his twice broken nose was a constant reminder that he needed to take these threats seriously. Still, with his motto, "When the good run from the bad, the bad win," ringing in his ears, he couldn't afford to cower behind closed doors at every threat.

The warden did not miss Patrick's tone, and it irritated him and his security chief, who was listening in on another prison extension. After all, the warden was going out of his way to warn Patrick, something he didn't make a habit of doing. But over the years Patrick had proven to be both a friend and a trustworthy ally. The warden had called him in at different times during the day or night when it seemed that riots might break out, and Patrick had come in to help resolve the conflicts before tensions took over the always volatile atmosphere in his prison.

"Listen, my friend," the warden said with conviction, "this time you must take the threat seriously."

"OK, let me have it," Patrick replied with more attention.

"We've heard that El Pato wants you dead," the director answered. Patrick was not surprised. El Pato's trial for the murders of Carlitos' family had not gone well, at least as far as El Pato himself was concerned; he had done what he could in his attempts to bribe and intimidate witnesses, but he had not been able to get to little Carlitos, the main eyewitness to the crimes. The little boy's videotaped testimony had been very damaging to El Pato's case. The boy had been able to identify him as the man who shot him and the rest of his family. The verdict had been guilty, the sentence death, and unless he won his appeal through some miracle or managed to escape, El Pato knew his time was coming to an end. It was an outcome he had not expected. In his arrogance, he had truly come to believe he was above the law and immune from punishment.

"Even now, he isn't facing reality," the warden told Patrick. "What he's doing instead is focusing all of his anger and fear on you. He sees you as the cause of his troubles, and he's offering to give a motorcycle to anyone who does him the favor of killing you. Crazy as it is," the warden added, "you know he has friends out there. He's not lacking for people who can be bought."

After hanging up, Patrick thought long and hard about what to do next, then once again he called his friend back in Bismarck, Sheriff Bob Harvey. After hearing him out, Harvey outlined a list of security measures he thought Patrick should follow for the next several months.

Even as he tried to ignore that danger, Patrick had to deal with other, and in some ways even more sinister, threats. As he and The GOD'S CHILD Project gained more and more publicity across the United States and internationally, Patrick attracted more and more attention from individuals who hoped to find in him the answers to all of their problems, or from those who decided for whatever reason that he was to blame for their personal troubles. Even to his family and friends, Patrick rarely spoke publicly about these incidents, and his small staffs in

Bismarck and Guatemala worked continuously to shield him from the occasional threat or potential risk.

During an earlier interview, Patrick said that he believed he would never be free from that kind of threat. "There are a lot of wounded birds out there," he said, "and unfortunately, some of them turn to violence, some to a more insidious kind of crime."

He talked about all of the times he has been harassed by crank phone calls, has received threatening letters, or been forced to fend off advances from people whom many might consider to be unbalanced.

I wondered whether he ever became angry about it.

"Of course, but it also makes me sad," he answered, "because those who threaten me are hurting, and they need our help and prayers." He talked about the woman who, after reading about Patrick and his work, quit her job in California and traveled to Guatemala, convinced that God had appeared to her in a dream, telling her that she was destined to be the mother of Patrick's children.

Another time, on a speaking tour through the United States, he received a late-night telephone call from a man who claimed to be a member of a racist group, threatening violence against Patrick's brown-skinned son, who was with him on the trip.

Four times he changed residences in Guatemala when former prisoners or disturbed individuals living on the streets found out where he lived, and scaled walls or otherwise tried to force their way into his family home.

In one 12-month period he and his son were forced to move three times from small apartments he maintained in Bismarck because a woman with a history of mental health problems began stalking him, banging on doors and windows late at night, damaging the project's car, and throwing human waste through his open apartment windows. He eventually moved his family into a high-security apartment building in Bismarck.

In 1997, Patrick welcomed to the project a retired couple from the United States, who said they wanted to volunteer. Several months later, Patrick was forced to suspend, and then eventually fire, this couple for misconduct, although Patrick offered to help these volunteers to find a new project to work with, or to help them to get back home. Instead of accepting his offer, they left that day, vowing that they would do everything in their power to destroy Patrick. Their hope, they said, was to kill the project by destroying its founder and leader.

Once again Patrick found himself the victim of a vicious rumor campaign. Initially, he responded by instructing his worried staff and volunteer team to ignore the rumors and insinuations, reminding them that, "Christ had to endure much worse." Patrick's hope was that this couple would move on and find a new outlet for their energies, but he could not have been more wrong.

On June 2, 1998, five weeks after he had first suspended this volunteer couple, he received a phone call informing him that he was about to be arrested.

"For what?" he inquired incredulously. The caller didn't know, but encouraged Patrick to act quickly. Calling the project's attorney and three older boys, Patrick drove into Guatemala City and walked straight into the District Attorney's office. "I hear you're looking for me," he said.

The government workers were astounded. Never before had they had someone accused of crimes so horrible simply walk right in and say, "Here I am." Patrick learned that during the previous five weeks, the fired couple and two of their Guatemalan friends had traveled around the country, making dozens of different accusations against Patrick. These included allegations of illegal adoptions, drug abuse, child abuse, theft, kidnapping—even trafficking in body parts.

Unlike 1991, when Patrick had first returned to Guatemala alone and without resources, this time he knew he had to fight back. He told friends that he believed in forgiving his enemies, but not too quickly. For the sake of the program's poor, he said he had to stop the damage they were causing, and halt their efforts to have him falsely imprisoned in Guatemala for years, possibly for the rest of his life.

After extensive investigations, Patrick was cleared of each of the numerous accusations that this couple and their Guatemalan friends had made against him. The Guatemalan District Attorney's office, supported by various human rights groups, decided instead to criminally charge the two Guatemalans for making false accusations. They were arrested and imprisoned, but the American couple had already fled the country. They promised to return to Guatemala to testify at the criminal trial of their two Guatemalan friends, but never went back. Alone and defenseless, both Guatemalans were tried, convicted and sentenced to pay high fines and serve three years in prison for making their false claims.

Patrick, pained at the damage they had done to him, nevertheless told the press, "We look forward to forgiving our enemies and, yes, we will help these two people in prison too."

Still wanted by Guatemalan authorities for questioning in a separate case, the former volunteer couple moved farther south into South America, where they volunteered with a different charity, while continuing to carry on their international slander campaigns against Patrick and his worldwide efforts. After winning a series of highly-lauded, history-making court cases in Guatemala, Central America, that established the rights of the falsely accused to defend their good names in court, in July 2003, Patrick and The GOD'S CHILD Project Board of Directors filed suit against this couple in United States District Court. This case was eventually settled on very favorable terms, with acknowledgements, apologies and large financial settlements to both Patrick and the Project. Patrict gave his share to charity. The GOD'S CHILD Project used its share to improve and pay down debt on the Project's Santa Madre Homeless Shelter; Central America's only year-round homeless shelter open to those in need.

Through it all, Patrick continued his work, and the project continued to grow and thrive, but in a letter to a friend, he expressed his private pain and anger.

"Sometimes in my darkest moments, usually late at night when I'm trying to forget the day's pressures and simply go to sleep, I question God about this. Why, when I'm working so hard to help the poor, does He allow this kind of thing to happen to me, not just once, but over and over again? But then I tell myself that the earlier experiences were what tempered me to face this one. They were a gift, really, because had I not learned that this kind of overwhelming pain is survivable, I think I would have crumbled under the pressure. As it is, I simply cannot, I simply will not, allow the bad to win."

CHAPTER EIGHTEEN

Excerpt from a television interview

When everything is said and done, nothing that I have ever done has been of my own creation, since it has been for the poor and for God's kingdom. All of the requests, inspirations and skills to get the job done have come from God.

When we suffer because we said "yes" to God's request, He suffers with us and is even closer at our side. When we rejoice, He rejoices too, though in all honesty we really can't rightfully take any of the credit ourselves.

At any time we can say, "I've had enough" and stop doing the special work that God wants us to do. The nobility of our faith, the definition of our desire for sanctity, however, comes in our persistence in saying, "yes."

—Patrick Atkinson, 2002

Patrick has never heard of Malawi. He tells me he doesn't even know what continent it's on, although he assumes Africa. He pulls out an atlas and takes a look. It is indeed in Southern Africa. The reason he needs to know, is because he's received a letter from Ted Sneed, a man he met years earlier at an international conference in Antigua. Sneed had worked for

UNICEF and was now working closely with the United Nations.

Sneed's request on the surface seems simple. He is asking Patrick to come to Malawi, to assess the situation of street children there, and to recommend an approach for providing assistance to them. It is the kind of work that Patrick has done for years. But one line of the letter stands out and makes Patrick shiver. "Malawi has between 300,000 and 360,000 HIV/AIDS orphans. Life expectancy has dropped from 48 years to 39 years in the last decade. Infant and child mortality rates are among the highest in the world." A quick Web search tells Patrick that nearly 40 percent of the adult population in Malawi is infected with the HIV virus, and will die within three years. That means an exploding orphan population in a society that is not used to street children. Sneed explains in his letter that family ties have always been important in Malawi. For generations, when children were orphaned, the extended families took them in. Now, though, it is different. With so many adults dying of AIDS, there are cases in which all of the adults in the family are sick or have already died. Those who remain are simply overwhelmed, with no way to provide for all of the children who are being orphaned. So, these children end up living on the streets. The problems in Africa seemed insurmountable.

"God, I can't do this," Patrick says, and then he outlines all of the reasons it's a bad idea to get involved. After all, he has more than enough work to do right here in Guatemala, he says, and the project's resources are already overextended. The GOD'S

CHILD Project is growing at an explosive rate, and Patrick can't imagine how he can work any more hours than he already is. Just keeping in touch with benefactors and coordinating the efforts of international volunteers is overwhelming. Besides, Patrick says, he's always thought that when it was time to grow the project, the natural progression would be to establish similar programs in other Central American countries first. El Salvador seemed like the next logical move. And besides all of that, he confides, the last place he really wants to go, is Africa. He will decline.

But before he can even post the refusal letter, he receives a second request, this time from Chikondi Mpokosa, the head of child rights and advocacy in Blantyre, Malawi, a man who works directly with the orphans themselves. Without some sort of help, the letter states, these children stand no chance at all.

"I know you have built up a wealth of experience in this area," writes Mpokosa. "We would like to network and learn as much as possible...we would be so grateful."

With the second request now before him, Patrick feels a pull that he can't resist. Before the day is out, he will begin making travel arrangements. He's not happy about it, but still, he makes the call to his board of directors, informing them of his decision to consider expanding into Malawi. With their blessing, he would leave within the month for Africa, to assess the situation.

ZOMBA, MALAWI, AFRICA
July 30, 2001

Malawi reminded Patrick of Eastern Montana. Flat scrub brush and farm fields as far as the eye could see. He had spent the morning touring the countryside with Fr. Ignatius Sudwedi and Bishop Chamgwera of Zomba, Malawi, traveling from one shelter to another. Patrick was trying to get a feel for how the African system worked. He knew from experience that it was better to work within a country's existing system than to try to reinvent the wheel. It would be easier to simply scrap many of the weak, corrupt and inefficient systems he had seen over the years, but he knew that if he couldn't get the local leaders to feel a sense of ownership, they were sure to fail.

Patrick's hope was to set up a basic school and orphanage program for the AIDS orphans in Malawi, and then administer it from Bismarck and Guatemala, the way he did the other charities that operated under The GOD'S CHILD Project umbrella. He would use the Internet to follow the children's progress and the work of the project's volunteers in Malawi. But Patrick was quickly learning that rural Africa was too desperate and poor to supply even the most basic of services. Electricity was rare and telephone lines were even more of a luxury. As in most developing countries, cellular phone services were much more common, since they didn't require the huge investments that traditional phone services needed. E-mail could not be counted on here, he knew, and where it was available it was very expensive at $5 a minute.

Deep in thought and wondering how he could make an effective, low-cost program work for thousands of orphaned children, Patrick's attention was suddenly diverted by hand-waving children alongside the road, jumping up and down to attract attention and waving long sticks at the passing motorists.

"What is that?" Patrick asked his hosts.

"Fried rat on a stick," Fr. Suwedi replied casually.

"No," Patrick said. "Are you kidding?"

"Seriously. Those kids are our equivalent of your fast food hamburger places," he added with a laugh. "Except here the kids start a field on fire, the mice and rats run into their nests and the grass burns off. Then the kids go out, reach down into the nests, catch the rats, skewer them and roast them."

"They're not bad. Perhaps you'd like to try one?" said the bishop with a twinkle in his eye.

The shelters and clinics they visited that day were for different groups—orphaned girls and boys, abandoned or widowed mothers, pregnant women, adults and teenagers slowly dying of AIDS.

"The way we like to work in Central America," Patrick explained, "is to rely heavily on our foster parents to raise the kids. I never like to institutionalize orphaned kids, because I think it's a lousy way for a child to grow up. So we pay the foster families to raise the boys and girls, keep them fed and help them do well in school. It's a system that works pretty well there. But I can see that we need to do something different here," Patrick added after he had seen how serious the orphan crisis was in Africa.

"Yes," the bishop agreed. "Here, any family that can take in orphaned children has already done so—the children of their own brothers, sisters and cousins. There are very few households that have remained untouched by the AIDS epidemic."

"So we'd have to run some sort of shelter," Patrick said thinking aloud, "but the emphasis would have to be on education." What he really needed to do first, he realized, was to decide how he could efficiently run a new program half a world away, and one that was significantly different from those that the volunteers and small staff were running in Guatemala.

As he studied the problem, Patrick prayed for help. He just wasn't sure what to do. Everywhere he went, Bishop Chamgwera, Fr. Suwedi and Patrick saw the sunken cheeks and emaciated bodies of AIDS victims and realized the enormity of the undertaking they faced. Here in Africa, Patrick realized, victory would have to be measured one child at a time, one task at a time. Otherwise the work would seem hopeless.

"It is easy to give in to hopelessness and despair here," Bishop Chamgwera agreed. "These people used to have such joy in them. Now shadows are everywhere, even in their souls. Yet, what else can we do? We must receive each of these children as Christ. We need to teach them all. Helping us learn how to do that is where you come in, Patrick."

The size of the challenge they faced became more and more evident while Patrick was there. Medical care was available in the bigger cities like Zomba and Blantyre, but even there the doctors were overwhelmed by the AIDS epidemic that was slowly killing the African continent. In the outlying areas they could see that simply finding first aid was an almost impossible challenge.

The day he departed Malawi, Patrick sat alone on the hard plastic bench at the Blantyre airport and reflected on all that he had seen over the past several days. Never before, even in the violence of the war in Central America and the stifling poverty of Southeast Asia, had he witnessed such despair in the faces of those among whom he had walked.

His thoughts were transported back a dozen years, to the letters from Guatemalan street children, begging him to return. He remembered how he had felt then, after trying unsuccessfully to get the children off the streets and into shelters so that he could return to the United States. He couldn't ignore those cries for help, and he didn't feel he could ignore this one either.

"Give me some direction, God" he prayed again. "I can't do the work if I don't know where we are supposed to start."

Before returning to North Dakota, Patrick decided to visit with a friend who was now a missionary in Kisii, near the Tanzanian border. He had first met Evan Beauchamp when the two of them worked the streets of New York City together, back in the early 1980s. Both were driven by an almost burning desire to serve God and the poor, and it was this desire that had taken them both to Guatemala as missionaries, and now to Africa.

Evan met Patrick at the Nairobi international airport. After buying some provisions at a local store and meeting another friend, they hopped into Evan's Toyota Landcruiser and drove seven hours to Kisii. There they spent the night, and early the next morning they headed out on a five-day visit to the Serengetti Game Reserve in Tanzania. Their daytime hours were spent searching for the African wildlife that Patrick wanted to see and photograph. Evan, who was 25 years older than Patrick and was now in his third mission stay in Africa, seemed to know where to find all of the animals that tourists like to photograph. They saw elephants, giraffes, zebras and a lion. At night in their hotel, the men sat around bamboo tables on a stone patio overlooking Lake Victoria and sharing stories of their shared times together, and the times that they had been apart.

Three days into their trip, they got a flat tire on a dusty, deserted road. At first, it seemed like a minor inconvenience. Well used to the vehicle breakdowns that the Guatemalan project's pig truck had subjected him to almost daily, Patrick told Evan he'd take care of the problem. They argued about it for a moment, but once the car was on the jack, Evan stepped aside and allowed Patrick to take over. Patrick dropped to both knees and placed one hand on both sides of the flat tire to take it off.

Without warning, the mission's old tire jack failed and the heavily-loaded truck sank down into the dusty road. Patrick's hands were under the metal frame of the sinking truck. He couldn't move his left hand in time and it became trapped under the deflated tire as the Landrover fell.

At the same time, the tire rim was cutting through the rubber tire and into Patrick's fingers as the weight of the vehicle crushed his hand. He cried out in pain and also fear because he could see that if the truck shifted even a little in the wrong direction, the wheel rim would slice his fingers off. He could see small streams of blood soaking into the sand of the road.

Evan ran to Patrick and pulled at his trapped hand. "No, no, stop," Patrick commanded through gritted teeth. Evan then ran to the other side of the Land Cruiser and climbed inside, intending to start the truck and drive it forward. The added weight of Evan in the truck caused Patrick to scream in pain, and when he realized what Evan was intending to do, he yelled at him to stop, knowing that the tires would spin in the sand and amputate his fingers..

"Get behind the car and push it off," Patrick cried.

Evan stood alongside the truck and reached as far as he could inside. The truck was firmly in gear, and he couldn't reach the clutch. "Sorry, old man," Evan said in distress, "but I'm going to have to climb back inside and take it out of gear." Evan lifted his 200-pound body into the driver's seat and Patrick nearly passed out as that weight shifted onto the tire rim. Evan shifted the car into neutral and crawled out. He got behind the truck and tried to roll it forward but it refused to budge.

Not sure what to do next, Evan sent up a prayer. Then, opening his eyes, he looked down the road, and saw a group of 20 or so school children walking toward them. They had been let out of school early that day they later told Evan in Swahili, and they were on their way to the market. Evan called to them, explaining what the problem was. Lining up the children behind the truck, Evan yelled at Patrick to take a deep breath, and then he ordered the crowd of school kids to push. They did in one tremendous effort, and together they managed to roll the car off Patrick's trapped hand. Patrick pulled away and rolled down the road's embankment. He couldn't remember ever being in more pain. His fingers were immediately swollen to twice their size, they were purple, deeply gashed and throbbing. Evan realized the seriousness of the situation. Their truck was useless, their jack was broken and the tire was still flat—and they were in the middle of Tanzania, with no phone or radio. The nearest hospital was hundreds of miles away.

God granted them another favor. One of the school boys noticed a motorcycle driving in the distance. "Shout!" Evan said to the kids. "Shout and wave your hands." Within a minute or two they managed to flag down the passing motorcyclist. It turned out to be Nigel, the owner of the hotel on the shore of Lake Victoria where Patrick and Evan were staying. Nigel had lived in the Tanzanian outback and was a frequent witness to medical emergencies. He used Patrick's shirt like a tourniquet to stop the flow of blood, then loaded Patrick onto the back of his motorcycle. Fearful that he would pass out from pain, exhaustion and shock, he then tied Patrick to his own body and placed his own helmet on Patrick's head.

"Ride like this," Nigel commanded, thrusting Patrick's hand straight up in the air. Patrick did, but even with the shirt tied around his hand, blood streamed down his bare, scratched arm. His fingers were stretched and shiny from the extreme swelling, and the motorcycle's speed created a breeze on the exposed nerves. Patrick felt faint from the pain.

When they finally reached the hotel, Nigel's wife took one look at the hand and shook her head. There wasn't much she could do here, she said, except to open several bottles of ice-cold water. She poured the purified water into a basin and told Patrick to soak his hand in that to decrease the swelling and clean the wound.

Nigel, in the meantime, used the hotel's radio-phone to place a call to Doctors Without Borders. No doctors were available, but they suggested an alternative—Angels on Wings. A doctor from that group was willing to fly down from Nairobi, Kenya, several hundred miles away, but he said the cross-border trip would take massive amounts of paperwork and a lot of time to arrange. In the meantime, they did an over-the-phone evaluation. Their conclusion was that Patrick had suffered skin and tissue trauma, and quite possibly broken bones. But short of fixing a compound fracture there was little they'd be able to do outside of a hospital if and when they did get there. They recommended ice, antibiotics and painkillers, which were available at the hotel, and a wait-and-see approach.

It turned out to be the correct approach. Later that night, the swelling began to subside, and over the next several days Patrick's hand steadily improved. As he flexed his stiff fingers he said to Evan, "The fact that this hand still works is nothing short of a miracle."

"There's a silver lining in this cloud," Evan replied. "You have just learned first hand one of the major problems of the work you're contemplating in Africa. Access to simple medical care is going to be a challenge." Patrick just groaned.

Several days later, as Patrick sat on an airplane flying back to North Dakota, he had to two-finger type a basic business plan for setting up a mission in Africa. He had made an important decision. He had made an arrangement with an already established boarding school, and had given them the go-ahead for the bishop to begin accepting perhaps 200 of the neediest AIDS-orphaned kids. Now Patrick just had to figure out how he was going to pay the bills. His core belief was still very basic; if this was God's work, then God would inspire people to help. Now he just had to trust in the divine, and use his acute business skills to figure out how God was going to make this happen.

As his flight lay over at London's Heathrow Airport,

Patrick called his office manager, Mandy Schaaf, in Bismarck, to tell her about his injury and ask her to book an appointment with his doctor.

"Oh, and while you're at it," he added, "I was also bitten by a tse-tse fly, so I should probably have a blood test to check for sleeping sickness." He mentioned it almost as an afterthought. With everything else that had happened in Tanzania, the fact that he had been bitten on the neck by an African fly and that the bite on his neck had swollen to the size of a golf ball didn't seem that important.

Later that week, the first week in August 2001, he consulted with The GOD'S CHILD Project's board of directors and then announced to his staff, and later to the project's supporters and the media, that The GOD'S CHILD Project was expanding into Africa.

He had no way of foreseeing the dark cloud that was already gathering on the world's horizon.

ANTIGUA, GUATEMALA
Sept. 11, 2001

Patrick began Sept. 11, 2001, like any other day. He was up at 7 a.m., and as usual, turned on CNN En Español before hopping into the shower. He did this every morning because it gave him a chance to hear what was going on in the world while he got ready for work. When he turned off the water, he picked up an unusual tone to the news. He was still toweling off his hair when he heard a horrifying news story. Still rubbing the towel over the top of his head, he left the bathroom and went to stand in front of the living room television screen. He didn't move a muscle for the next 20 minutes.

"We heard a big bang," one eyewitness said, "and everybody started running out, and we saw the plane had hit one side of the tower, and there was smoke everywhere. People were jumping out of windows. And then I saw another plane hit. Oh, my God!"

Patrick watched in horror along with the rest of the world, as New York City's World Trade Center Towers fell. He couldn't drag himself away as the video was broadcast over and over again. It was just after 9 a.m. on the American East Coast, so he was seeing the events after they had happened. He watched as people ran from the mushroom cloud that formed when the buildings collapsed. He saw people jump from the burning towers. He realized, finally, that he was still mindlessly toweling off hair that had long since dried. Waking up to the situation, he dressed quickly and hopped in his car to drive to the office. Some of his staffers were just arriving and many had not yet heard about the terrorist attacks on New York's Twin Towers or the Pentagon in Virginia. Patrick gathered them together and they went to The Dreamer Center's Walsh Family Hall where they watched the news events of the century unfold for several hours.

For the first few days after 9/11, Patrick felt paralyzed. With all of his worldwide travels and experience, he had realized what many around him had not yet grasped; that the events of Sept. 11 were world-changing, and that they were the start of unrest that would heap more misery on the world's poorest people. He knew that his job and the jobs of everyone who worked with the poor and suffering, were about to become infinitely more difficult.

Patrick had lived through crises before. He knew that quick action was necessary. But he felt as if he were moving in slow motion. He knew that if he was going to save The GOD'S CHILD Project from the financial crisis that he was sure was about to follow, there were steps he needed to take right away, but he couldn't focus. His mind kept replaying the awful events of that day.

The tough times that he had predicted came almost immediately. Donations to The GOD'S CHILD Project dried up almost overnight. People were grieving and distracted. Many diverted their normal charitable giving to the many 9/11 charities that had been set up virtually overnight. Because his small project operated on a shoestring and was just starting to come out of the normal summertime donation doldrums, it didn't take more than a few days for the project to hit red ink.

Patrick understood people's feelings of inertia, because he was feeling it too. He called emergency staff and board meetings for his programs in Guatemala, but found he couldn't focus long enough to prepare for them. He had nightmares that disturbed his sleep; and while he couldn't always remember them the next day, they left him feeling uneasy. He tried to pray, but found his mind drifting off.

His friends and coworkers noticed the change in him. Rev. Lisa Ahlness, president of The GOD'S CHILD Project North Central Board of Directors, expressed her concern to fellow board members:

> Patrick seems lost since the bombings. He can't concentrate on the writing projects at hand, etc. He's very worried about "what's going to happen." And although he's normally a very happy, positive and upbeat person, he seems to be fighting off a depression-like funk. He has lived through too many wars, he says, and he does NOT want to go through the war thing again."

Patrick did his best to reassure all of those who were depending on him, but privately, he wrote to friends:

> "I don't know what it is that's affecting me so deeply and on so many levels, but since the bombings I have been absolutely frozen. Can't focus. Can't move ahead. I go to bed late because I'm not tired and I get up exhausted, regardless of how much I've slept…and unlike before when I was able to focus on three or four things at the same time, with this I am directionless. I have all of the desire to move past it, but without the energy to go forward or the knowledge of which direction I should move in. I'm spending a lot of time in prayer and thought, but both are forced and seem to be of little value."

From his small office in The Dreamer Center, Patrick saw that The GOD'S CHILD Project was quickly going broke. The project was losing $1,800 a day, and donations were off 80 percent over anticipated income. At that rate, he knew he would be cutting programs within weeks and then shutting the doors within a few months. If the project that he and so many others had worked so hard to build was going to survive, he knew he had to snap out of this crippling depression and take immediate steps.

Seven days after 9/11, Patrick's first order of business was to stabilize the situation in Guatemala the best he could. Though it broke his heart to do it, he laid off about one-third of his Guatemalan staff, satisfied that he had been able to find jobs for each of them elsewhere. He trimmed other expenses in the project wherever he could, while publicly vowing that not a single child would be dropped from The GOD'S CHILD Project program. In Africa, hoped-for funding from the United Nations was first suspended and then cancelled entirely, so the project that he'd been starting up in Malawi was limited to the 35 children who had already been accepted into his care.

Patrick felt in his heart that God did not want him to abandon the African effort, but expanding the program there was no longer a priority. Survival was. By the end of that seventh day after 9/11, Patrick had arranged a flight to the United States to start making direct appeals for help.

Volunteers held special drives in North Dakota and

elsewhere and he went on the speaking circuit, talking at churches, civic groups and club meetings. He called in to radio talk shows and spoke on TV programs, pleading with benefactors to break from the frozen stance which he too had shared, and to start living and giving again. He laid it all out in spoken word as well as on paper, and explained to benefactors around the nation what would happen to mom-and-pop charities like The GOD'S CHILD Project if they withdrew their support even for a short period of time. He wrote:

Twenty days ago, something very wrong, something very evil happened to our country and to our people. It was wrong to the degree that human words cannot express. Someday we will have to look to the mystics and the poets to express our shared suffering, as today there is little that can be adequately said...this violence is now threatening to end, to close down, all that we have worked so hard to build. The goal of terrorism is to cause destruction by causing fear and a disruption of our normal lives, and we must not allow the terrorists to further achieve their goal by allowing them to destroy the heart of our nation; our local charities and charitable efforts...

Patrick's message and endless efforts worked. Donations began to come in again, in small $10 and $20 amounts. But it wasn't enough. Patrick kept asking, and kept praying, doing his best not to give in to defeat.

"It's as if the rest of the world is as frozen as I was," he told another group. "But we can't stop living: 2,500 kids don't stop eating, going to school, and ripping holes in their jeans. God will help us."

At an annual dinner held for The GOD'S CHILD Project in Bismarck at the end of November 2001, Patrick shared a success story with his audience:

"I probably shouldn't tell you this, but two days ago I over-drafted a check. It was scholarship day in Guatemala, which means that 2,583 kids show up at the Dreamer Center with their grades in hand, waiting for their monthly tuition and foster care room and board check. Without it, a lot of these kids don't eat. So, before I left Guatemala yesterday, I went ahead and wrote the checks. They came to a total of $12,600. When I emailed Mandy Schaaf and Nancy Feist in our Bismarck office that I had done this, there was an ominous silence on their end. They simply didn't know what to say, except that the money just wasn't there to cover these checks. That was two days ago."

"Tonight, as I was dressing to come and speak to you, Nancy Feist called on the phone to say that today we received an anonymous donation—a bequest from somebody's estate. The check had been written out four days ago and sent in to our office. It was for the amount of $12,600."

On the day that Carlitos left Bismarck to return home to Guatemala, he was accompanied to the city's airport by dozens of well-wishers, and more than a few tears were shed by the people who had grown to love this little boy over the past several weeks. They knew that he was returning to live with his cousin and his extended family, and they hated to see him go back to a life of poverty. More than one family had asked Patrick about the possibility of adopting Carlitos, a request to which Patrick had been required to respond with a definite "No.'"

"First of all, I promised I would take him back," Patrick told one couple. "And secondly, he has an extended family that loves him and is waiting for him to come home. He belongs with them, because that's who he is. We can give him many, many things, but they will give him a sense of belonging, of family, and a history of who he is. They also love him as much as we do—probably more. Who knows? It just may be this love that is going to help him to someday make sense out of all the terrible things that have happened to him."

As his new friends waved goodbye Carlitos turned and walked through the door and down the jetway. Under one arm, he carried a brand new set of toy trucks, and in the other he held a plush and now well-worn teddy bear. He turned once to look back and uttered a single word: "Gracias."

In Bismarck life returned to normal for the nearly 100 people who had lined up to help Carlitos. The doctors and nurses took on new cases, his host family and new friends went back to their daily routines. The GOD'S CHILD Project moved on to help other children. But the legacy of Carlitos and the love he generated live on.

On a return trip to Antigua in 2003, I visited Carlitos. He is healthy now. He attends school sometimes, although his cousin does not see the importance of it and does not insist. On many days, Carlitos finds better things to do. When The GOD'S CHILD Project workers visit their home, cousin Luis can't really explain why his children have stopped coming to The Dreamer Center to take advantage of the programs offered there—the clothing, food and medical care—or why he has not moved his family into the new house that project volunteers built just for them. The house sits empty, with weeds growing up around the door that volunteers had painted a bright blue. The color is fading a little. The neighbors living around it shake their heads at the waste. It is not a perfect, happy ending.

And yet, Patrick insists that he will not give up on Carlitos. He takes comfort from the fact that the little boy is vibrant and healthy, and seems happy playing with his friends in the streets of Altotenango. If you ask Carlitos what he wants to be when he grows up, he smiles and says "a doctor." It is Patrick's hope that The GOD'S CHILD Project can help Carlitos make his dream come true.

AFTERWORD

Patrick frequently thinks of his sister's mirror, that illusionary magical hallway with its limitless number of exits, each door representing a different direction his life might have taken, or could still take. After all, he is still a young man. He still dreams of that house overlooking the river, a wife and kids. But then he remembers all of the times he might have given up, only to be bailed out at the last moment, and he knows that his life has a particular purpose. Someday, he says, God might decide he's done enough, and can retire. But he doubts it.

Today, The GOD'S CHILD Project is helping children and families in Guatemala, El Salvador, Malawi and in the United States. Patrick oversees that aid as the head of The GOD'S CHILD Project International, traveling four times a year to Africa. His work was recognized in 2005 when he was awarded the Guatemalan National Congressional Medal of Honor.

The poor still surround him wherever he goes. His enemies are still there, too. Though El Pato was convicted for the murders of Carlitos' family and remains on death row, Patrick still receives the occasional death threat. His God is stronger.

"Whenever I hear about another child in trouble," he explains, "I close my eyes, say a prayer, and leap. For God, we should give all."

The GOD'S CHILD Project

Since its founding in Bismarck, N.D., by Patrick Atkinson in 1991, The GOD'S CHILD Project has grown to comprise an international family of distinct grass-roots charities:

The GOD'S CHILD Project (International) coordinates all inter-project efforts, supports and trains nonprofit efforts around the world, with national and international health, education, community development, and human rights protection campaigns, and handles the program's charitable efforts in Malawi, Africa. Patrick Atkinson is the Executive Director of GCP (I), www.godschild.org.

The GOD'S CHILD Project North Central is based in Bismarck, N.D., and raises awareness and funds for and oversees the project's efforts in Guatemala and the Upper Midwest region of the United States. It shares in the care and education of children in Africa. Jena Gullo is the Executive Director of GCPNC, www.GCPNC.org.

The GOD'S CHILD Project South Central is based in Irving, Texas, and raises awareness and funds for and oversees the project's efforts in El Salvador and the Southern Central region of the United States. It shares in the care and education of children in Africa. Pete Miller is the Executive Director of GCPSC, www.GCPSC.org.

The GOD'S CHILD Project Foundation is based in Bismarck, N.D., and works independently of the project to develop a long-term endowment to support the works of all GCP programs. Randy Bakke is the President of GCPF, www.GCPF.org.

DOMUS is a separate non-profit charity founded to provide affordable housing for the world's homeless, and to support nonprofit groups that help the homeless. Patrick Atkinson is the Executive Director of DOMUS.

Patrick Atkinson founded the Institute for Trafficked, Exploited & Missing Persons (ITEMP) as a research, public education, and social action organization to fight against contemporary slavery. Since its founding and by working through GOD'S CHILD Project-founded or supported programs, ITEMP has become Central America's largest non-governmental anti-human trafficking program. Atkinson travels tens of thousands of miles each year giving anti-human trafficking presentations. www.ITEMP.org

Patrick Atkinson was the founder or co-founder of each of these charitable efforts, as well as dozens of charities in Central America, Southeast Asia, and Africa. He resides in Bismarck, N.D., and Antigua, Guatemala, and travels over 125,000 miles each year as a guest preacher/speaker, and in his efforts to serve God and the poor.

HOW TO HELP

Help carry on Patrick's work with the poorest among us. Send checks, made payable to The GOD'S CHILD Project, to:

> The GOD'S CHILD Project
> 721 Memorial Highway
> P.O. Box 1573
> Bismarck, ND 58504

For more information, contact the GOD'S CHILD Project at 701-255-7956 or visit www.godschild.org.

ABOUT THE AUTHOR

Monica Hannan began her career in Bismarck as an intern in the KFYR-TV newsroom while in high school. After college, she worked at TV stations in Williston, N.D, and Twin Falls, Idaho. She returned to Bismarck in 1987 to take an anchor position at KFYR-TV, where she currently anchors the news at 5 p.m., 6 p.m. and 10 p.m. She also is the station's news director.

Monica has written two travel books with her husband: *Dakota Daytrips* and *More Dakota Daytrips*. They sold more than 28,000 copies. She also has written for magazines like *Home and Away*, *Historic Traveler* and *Dakota Catholic Action*, and has won numerous writing awards for fiction, non-fiction, and television reporting. In 2005, Monica was chosen Anchor of the Year by the North Dakota Broadcasters Association.

She is on the board of directors for Catholic Charities of North Dakota, The Bismarck Historical Society, and is a past board member for the GOD'S CHILD Project North Central.

Monica is a 1982 graduate of Minnesota State University, Moorhead, with degrees in history and mass communications. She also earned a master's in management from the University of Mary in 1990.

She is married to Cliff Naylor, a weatherman at KFYR. They are the parents of Meghanne, Clifford Jr. and Hannah.